D0064866

GRAND CENTRAL
PUBLISHING

LARGE
PRINT

ACT LiKE YOU GOT SOME SENSE

AND OTHER THiNGS MY DAUGHTERS TAUGHT ME

JAMIE FOXX

WITH NICK CHILES

GRAND CENTRAL
PUBLISHING

LARGE PRINT

Grand Central Publishing
Hachette Book Group
1290 Avenue of the Americas, New York, NY 10104
grandcentralpublishing.com
twitter.com/grandcentralpub

First Edition: October 2021

Grand Central Publishing is a division of Hachette Book Group, Inc. The Grand Central Publishing name and logo is a trademark of Hachette Book Group, Inc.

The publisher is not responsible for websites (or their content) that are not owned by the publisher.

The Hachette Speakers Bureau provides a wide range of authors for speaking events. To find out more, go to www.hachettespeakersbureau.com or call (866) 376-6591.

Library of Congress Control Number: 2021939255

ISBN: 9781538703281 (hardcover), 9781538703298 (ebook), 9781538719015 (large print), 9781538710913 (signed edition), 9781538710999 (special signed edition), 9781538722053 (special signed edition)

Printed in the United States of America

LSC-C

Printing 1, 2021

Dedicated to Estelle Marie Talley

CONTENTS

FOREWORD

BY
CORINNE FOXX

My dad (who I'm sure you know based on the cover of this book is Jamie Foxx) has led the most interesting life. He has laughed with sitting presidents, won numerous accolades, partied with the biggest names in hip-hop, chartered planes around the world—the list goes on and on. However, if you ask anyone who knows him, they would say what he talks about the most is not partying with Diddy or shaking hands with Obama. It's my latest acting performance, or how many points Anelise scored in her last basketball game. Being a father is one of my dad's greatest joys; it's apparent in everything that he does. He makes his entire world revolve around me and my sister. If he could spend every waking moment with us, he would—though my sister and I would desperately need some space. We're his pride and joy, and we feel that from him every day.

I think my dad wanted to write a book on fatherhood because when he started going through it, he had no blueprint on how to be a good father. He had to learn everything on the job, right in the moment. When I think of him at age twenty-six, holding me as a newborn, it must have been so intimidating for him. He had no idea what to do. But over the twenty-seven years of my own life, my father has been dedicated to figuring it out. He's always tried to get it right, even though his execution was unorthodox sometimes—not every dad is gonna hang out with his six-year-old at a topless pool. I feel like my dad wanted to write a book about fatherhood so he could share the lessons he's learned along the way. He can provide someone else with the map that he never got. I don't think this book is meant to portray Jamie Foxx as the perfect father. God knows, he got it wrong a lot of the time, as you will discover on these pages. But his intentions were always pure. I never once had to question if he was going to be there for me, if he would show up. I always knew I'd be the last thing he'd ever give up on.

I was excited to learn he was writing this book because I knew it would offer an honest, harsh but still delightful view on fatherhood. You don't need to be the perfect father; you don't even need to know what you're doing. The only thing that you have to do is try. Show up. Be there. Listen. My dad has always done those things—and my sister and I are better for it.

ACT LIKE YOU GOT SOME SENSE

PARENTING...
YOU AIN'T READY FOR IT

The first thing I learned about parenting is that the kids ain't going nowhere. When Corinne was born, the responsibility smacked me upside the head, made me scared as hell. It dawned on me that this parenting thing is forever. And it's not like having a puppy—the consequences of messing up are way worse than some shit on the carpet. When you take the kid to school on Monday, you actually have to get up and take them again on Tuesday. Damn, they got to go every day? The things you took for granted when you were a kid—like breakfast, lunch and dinner—that's now on you. No one is coming to make food for them.

But lemme slow down and introduce myself. Hello,

my name is Jamie. You may know me from film, television, stand-up comedy, the music world, being famous for my wild parties (which, by the way, are epic)—but there are two young girls in my life who don't give a shit about any of that and only know me as "Dad." Corinne is now twenty-seven, Anelise is thirteen. They have different mothers (don't judge me and I won't judge you).

Everything I learned about parenting came from Estelle Marie Talley and Mark Talley, the beautiful couple who adopted me at seven months. I consider them my grandparents because (and try to keep up because this story is messy) thirteen years before Mark and Estelle adopted me they had adopted my mother. Mark Talley was an uncle to my mother, Louise, whose family was the Rosebuds. From what I was told, my mother's mother, my biological grandmother, was stressed trying to raise my mom's other siblings. Believe me, I know how hard it is raising kids when you have money, and it's hard as fuck when you don't. So one day Estelle said to her, "I can't have kids because God didn't let me. I always wanted to have kids. Would you allow me to adopt Louise?" They agreed. I guess legally my mother is my sister—I know, it sounds like a country-ass Southern thing. But hey, I never married my cousin so, like I said, don't judge me.

My mother was thirteen when she moved to

Terrell, Texas, after spending her formative years in Dallas. Terrell was culture shock for her, to say the least. Dallas was a fast-moving city—not LA or New York, but certainly faster than Terrell, with its six stop lights. Though my mother moved begrudgingly, when she got there she was a star—beautiful, talented, charismatic. In high school she was the lead of the majorettes, strutting across the field with all eyes on her. Everybody wanted to be in her world.

But she never really took to Terrell, even though she was a big fish in a small pond. She yearned to get back to the hood in South Dallas, to what she knew. After high school graduation, she fled back there. By the time she turned twenty-six, she had gotten married to a man named Darrell Bishop and gave birth to a bighead boy named Eric Marlon Bishop. That was me. Their marriage didn't work out. My dad converted to Islam while my mother was pregnant, which immediately drove a wedge between them. The people I grew up with didn't have anything against Muslims, they just didn't understand the religion—the only thing they knew about Muslims was bow ties and bean pies. And have you ever been to the South? No disrespect to Muslims or Jews but WE EAT PORK. Pork chops, pork ribs...Fuck it, we put pork in our whiskey! Oh yeah, that's the other thing. Texans love to drink.

So my mother was having a hard time dealing

with that…and now add a newborn into the mix! Her family saw she was overwhelmed and offered lots of help. As a result, in my early months I would spend the majority of time in Terrell with my grandparents, Estelle and Mark. Finally, Estelle said to her daughter, "Why don't you let the boy stay here?" Soon that turned into, "Why don't you let me adopt the boy?"

I was five when I found out I was adopted. The news of my parentage was shocking—imagine learning who you thought was your sister was actually your mom and who you thought was your mother was your adoptive grandmother-slash-aunt-by-marriage (yeah, the story is complicated). But it didn't devastate me. This was a Black adoption—a kid is taken into a household by other family members, brought up with plenty of love and maybe somebody was getting a check in the deal. I had a family that cared for me. I was good. It didn't cave me in. The earth didn't stop spinning. I saw Joaquin Phoenix's *Joker* and shook my head when that dude choked his mom out with a pillow after he found out he was adopted.

Damn, bruh, did you have to kill her even after she took care of your silly ass?

Maybe that's the difference between white people and Black people—but then I learned Jack Nicholson also found out the woman he thought was his sister was actually his mother, and he turned out alright (he even has a few more Oscars than me, but I'm catching up). And he also played the Joker. Not sure what the connection is there but I think I should play the next Joker. There should be a Black Joker anyway, because he'd fuck Batman up and add some rims to his Batmobile. You know, hood shit, but I digress.

After I found out my grandparents weren't really my parents, I finally met my biological mother (as far as I knew, I had a sister who lived far away). I learned that she was not ready for the responsibility of parenting—I mean, I get it now, she was not ready to give up her youth, she was still out in them streets. But back then, I had a hard time with my mother being absent in my life. I got to see things from her perspective just a bit when my daughter Corinne was young and I sometimes had a rough time fitting fatherhood into my crazy schedule. Because I too was out in them streets. In fact, I still am sometimes.

One conversation that shifted my perspective was when I was chopping it up with my friend Phil and I told him I was tied up the next day because I had to "babysit" my kid. He corrected me and said, "No, you're not babysitting your kid, Black man, you're watching your child. When you 'babysit,' that's somebody else's kid. You got to lose that mindset."

I was a little embarrassed. "Oh, okay, yeah, not babysitting."

At this point, Corinne was living with her mother, Connie, but I still saw her plenty. I even got pretty good at doing her hair—although sometimes the other moms at her school had to intervene (but I was smart enough not to use Gorilla Glue). So anyway, this one time Connie had to work and had asked me to watch Corinne. I should preface this story by saying I'm a musician/actor/comedian and most of my work takes place late at night, often after most normal folks have gone to bed. That means I'm not a daytime person. In my mind, daytime is for sleeping. So, when I got to Connie's apartment, I was already sleepy as hell. Corinne was barely two at the time. I put a few toys in front of her and settled in on the couch.

"Just play with your toys, baby," I said. "I'm gonna be right here." I was right there—and I stayed there. I fell asleep. And when I woke up, my little bundle of joy had disappeared.

At first I thought, *Oh, she must have toddled into another room.* But as I searched the apartment and called her name, she was nowhere to be found. *Are you fuckin' kidding me?! I lost my daughter?!* The panic started to set in, real hard. My heart felt like a giant rock in my throat.

"Fuuuuck!" I yelled out loud.

Just as I was about to start having heart palpitations, I heard a knock on the door. When I opened it, the guy who lived down the hall was standing there with Corinne beside him. He also had two little kids of his own with him.

"Does this belong to you?" he said with a smirk on his face.

"Oh my God!" I said. "Get in here." Corinne started crying and yelling, "Noooo, not him!" I was thinking, *Damn, Corinne, what the hell? Making it look like I'm some abusive father?!* I snatched her up and brought her into the apartment, both angry and relieved. It was just horrible. I have no idea how long she was gone, but it's twenty-five years later and I'm still breaking out in cold sweats right now just recalling that afternoon. I was lucky; it could have been tragic, horrific.

But back to *my* childhood. While my mother was out there living in the fast lane, my grandparents were there for me. They were the opposite of my mom, who might say she was coming to see me next week, or on Christmas, and never show up—leaving me with painful longings that took many years to recover from. But I had my grandparents, and though many of my nights with my grandmother were pretty dull—they mostly consisted of sitting through *The Lawrence Welk Show*, which she loved—they didn't have to be exciting. I felt her love—even if I didn't love her television viewing tastes.

Jumping ahead to when I first became a dad, I had become too busy building this guy named Jamie Foxx, and it was messing up my relationship with my young daughter—running off to do stand-up, gone for weekend after weekend, and not physically being there. That was not the lesson I had learned from Estelle and Mark. I knew I had to do better.

And that's what this book is about. It's an assorted mix of stories about the lessons I learned— sometimes the easy way, more often the hard way— about parenting. Was I a perfect parent when I first had kids? No. Am I a perfect parent now? No. I'll probably look at this book in twenty years and be like *What the fuck was I thinking back then?* So why am I declaring myself some sort of authority on parenting? I'm not. *You* are, because you bought this fucking book. If you don't get anything else out of it, just be there for your dumbass kids. But, stay with me here, keep reading and maybe you'll learn a thing or two on what to do. Or not to do.

GRANNY

My grandparents told me they wanted me to have every tool in my toolbox—the educational tool, the artistic tool, the discipline tool, the moral tool. My grandmother wanted me to be worldly enough that I would be able to connect with any person in any room I walked into. She also wanted me to have a strong moral compass, because she knew when I moved away from Terrell and got out in the world, there would be many temptations and times when I needed to be able to say "No." Probably should've said no to a few movies, but you can take that up with my agent.

Granny wasn't above using every form of manipulation that she could conjure, wanting me to understand that the only way I would become special was through hard work. And sometimes, when I didn't want to practice the piano, she would actually break down in tears.

"I done did everything I can," she said through her sobs. "You just don't care."

I looked at her and felt the pain working its way through my chest. *Damn, bruh, you made Granny cry?*

"I don't want you to blow it," she said. "I don't want you to be here. I don't want you to be stuck here in Terrell."

I didn't completely understand what she was doing and saying, but I did sit my ass down at the piano and finish my lesson. My grandmother truly whipped me into shape, and to really understand me and how I look at the world, you need to get to know her.

Estelle Talley was the most influential figure in turning little nappy-headed Eric Bishop into the man I eventually became.

Granny was a tough lady... Basically, Granny was a badass bitch. Everybody in Terrell knew you better not step to Estelle with nothing "messy," as she liked to call it, unless you wanted to get your ass handed back to you. But she never looked scary and was always well put together—all this power was in a tidy little box with a bow. She was Madea long before Tyler Perry put on the pumps and the gray wig. But unlike in *Madea Goes to Jail*, Granny wasn't going to no jail, because the cops were scared of her too. She was a typical Taurus—which means she was blunt and stubborn as hell. A muumuu-wearing, .380-packing, churchgoing Taurus. With a little bit of cursing-your-ass-out on the side.

She showed me that there are ways to get away with always acting your truth. Her reason for being able to get away with it is that she practically raised our entire town.

For thirty years, she had her own nursery-school/day-care/can-I-just-leave-my-kids-here-for-a-minute-so-I-can-go-hang-with-my-boo place. The children at the nursery ranged from the white mayor's kids from across the tracks to the Black principal's kids from the southside. And me. She watched over us all and carried a very big stick—though when she thought I needed an ass-whupping, she usually handed that job to my grandfather (unfairly, I'd get more ass-whupping than other kids). She believed that a strong foundation of discipline allows young men and women to grow into strong, responsible adults.

There were many great days I remember at the nursery, running around with my little homies, playing games, watching television. Granny made sure we took care and respected ourselves, and that our bellies were full, even if we weren't entirely sure what they were full of. We spent a lot of time trying to figure out the mystery of the brownish-gray mush on Mystery Meat Mondays, but my grandmother was as tight-lipped as a KGB spy. Years later, she slipped up and finally told me the identity of the mystery meat: possum. Before you trip, let me say it wasn't bad. Very fatty, a little gamey. But we were country-ass kids—we wouldn't have cared.

For three decades, I would see the kids she raised grow up to be men and women—Black and white—and come to her for advice as they were figuring out how to raise their own kids. She never turned anyone away. But she didn't have no time for people coming around and being "messy," which meant engaging in any kind of behavior she thought was tacky, crude or dumb. If you were messy, she definitely let you know what was going on. Once I came home from college and I could hear my grandmother on the phone before I even got into the house.

"Well, bring your ass on over here and see if I don't shoot clean through yo ass!" she was saying to somebody.

When I walked in, she had her hand on her .380, which was resting on the table next to her. She slammed the phone down and looked up. Her anger quickly softened when she saw me.

"Granny, can you please give me the gun? You could have shot your grandson coming in here!"

"Yeah, well whoever coming in better be ready, 'cause I'm not having it today! It's one of them days."

When she got into it with her family, she wasn't one to hold back. Her toughness wasn't reserved for strangers, it was practiced on strangers so she could give family the full treatment. And, more importantly, since she dished it out, she could take it (which, of course, I carried with me into my comedy). I would hear different women in the family hitting her hard with things like, "Oh, you better be glad you married to Mark." Mark was the patriarch of the family—quiet, strong, dignified and respected. Everybody loved him; he was the epitome of what I like to call "Grown Man." They were trying to get at my grandma—it would be quite the accomplishment to win an argument against her—but she'd fire back twice as hard:

"You humpback bitches, I ain't scared of none of y'all. And I will see you at the reunion!"

And at the family reunions is where it would really go down. My grandmother was the best cook, but she was the exact opposite of Christlike about it. She'd stand over her food like Peter at the Pearly Gates.

"You ate enough of that!" she'd say when the family member she didn't like approached for seconds. "Put that down! Put that pie down."

"Granny, why you do that?" I once asked her.

"I ain't gonna let these fools eat all the good food," she said. "Uh-uh."

The way she would use her tears at the drop of a dime to get what she wanted, she would also use food. And goddamn, was she a mean cook. But it wasn't just what she cooked, she would hold sweets over my head if I wasn't behaving how she wanted. One of my enduring weaknesses is a fondness for sweet snacks—and because my grandma rarely let me have them, I'm still obsessed with them. I was also deprived of jelly back in the day. Sometimes we would have peanut butter, but never any jelly! Can you imagine? That's like spaghetti without meatballs, salt without pepper, Simon without Garfunkel—which would just be like a Bridge over Regular Water. I've since overcompensated and, to this day, when you open my refrigerator, all you see is bottles on top of bottles of delicious grape jelly. When the kids are at my house, they know to never, under any circumstance, touch my grape jelly, or else...Sometimes when I go in the refrigerator inside the pantry, I'll see that my stash has a big dent in it.

"Hey, I told y'all—nobody take my jelly!" I yell at them, but they ain't trying to hear me. I had to move to more drastic action—I set up a sting to catch them in the act. I waited down the hallway, out of sight.

From there, I could hear the refrigerator open in the middle of the night and I knew they were in there trying to get my stuff. At one in the morning! I hid out like that sheriff on the long highway that you didn't see when you were going 90 mph.

After the fridge opened, they scurried out with all kinds of snacks and sodas hidden in their clothes. I jumped out—to their screams. I lined them up and set out to frisking each one, finding loads of jellies and cupcakes and Reese's. All my stuff.

"Y'all eating bread and water for the rest of the week!"

Sorry, I got way too lost in that story. But I had a Snickers and I'm back on track talking about Granny.

I was the only child in the house, so my grandmother was my crew—a crew that didn't let me do shit. She liked to keep me busy and often made me do chores instead of playing with the other kids in the neighborhood. From my perspective, it seemed like her decisions were guided by one simple fact: She was a killjoy.

For example, when I was ten, if I looked out the window and saw the kids from the block playing outside, naturally I wanted to go out and play too. They weren't troublemakers, but I guess to my grandma they were, because they weren't encouraging me to do the dishes.

"Granny, they playin' across the street! Can I go over there?"

"Well, go on over there. See don't I cut your ass clean in two!"

"Granny, why you got to do that?"

"Go on, nigga. They can come over here but your ass ain't going nowhere." It was literally eighteen feet away.

I knew she didn't actually want to cut me clean in two, but I didn't want to test it.

At the ripe age of fifty-three, I now understand Granny. *Kinda.* She ended up teaching me discipline and that you can entertain yourself on your own side of the street. She didn't want anything bad to happen to me. But at the time, I just felt like she was being difficult as hell. I loved her though. In her mind, it came down to "That boy got something. I don't know what it is, but I don't want him to fuck it up hanging with them little badass kids down the street."

She ended up teaching me how to be a leader and not just a follower. You have your energy, you do your own thing and eventually the kids will come over and play with you—which they did. She told me she wanted me to learn how to enjoy my own space—in some backwards-ass way, but it worked. Now I don't chase the party. I create what I want and the right people find their way to me.

And she also taught me to be a leader by...well, being a leader herself. Even in small-town Texas, she was forward thinking. When I was in fifth grade, we were sitting in the pews on a Sunday afternoon listening to the reverend thunder from the pulpit of the local Baptist church.

"God created Adam and Eve," the reverend bellowed out. "He did not create Adam and Steve!"

Before the congregation could say "Amen," Estelle Talley rose up from her pew and yelled out, "You stop that!"

In the middle of the sermon. In the middle of the church. Smack dab in the middle of Texas. Nobody was gonna check Estelle Talley—including the reverend. The entire congregation probably stopped breathing. "You stop that!" she repeated. "God made sissies too. You stop preaching that!"

Now, I know the word "sissy" is hurtful to a lot of people, but please bear with me. This was Texas in 1976—we hadn't evolved yet and most of us didn't understand the connotations. But I will tell you this: Keep reading and you will see that Estelle Talley was most definitely an ally, even if she didn't have the right words for it at the time.

I don't know what the rest of the congregation was thinking, but I had no idea what she and the pastor were talking about. I had no concept of what gay was. Neither did the other kids. As on most

Sundays, we were just trying to get out in time for the football game. During his sermon, half the church was probably already thinking, *This dude is gonna make us miss the Cowboys!*

Granny's words were greeted with stunned silence. The preacher stared at her for several seconds. Then he changed the subject. Granny kept standing for a minute to let him know who was boss and then sat back down.

I never forgot what she said that day. A few years later, I asked her a question. "Granny, do you remember when you said, 'God made sissies too'?"

"Mm-hmm, I remember."

"What's that mean?"

"God made sissies," she repeated. "God made everybody on the planet. So when people trying to separate everybody, that don't make sense. We ain't here unless God said to be here." Like I said, I don't condone her use of the word "sissies" but I give her a pass for being old. Her heart was in the right place.

She told me that over the course of thirty years, she had raised many little boys in her preschool.

"I would raise little boys who like to play with army men, and I would raise little boys who like to play with dolls. Now, those little boys who like to play with dolls, being in Texas, they didn't know who to talk to, since the preacher talking crazy, so they would come talk to me. So I would protect them and their secrets."

She said she was trying to tell the reverend that he needed to "open the umbrella of Christianity."

"Open up the umbrella and let us all stand under it," she said. "Because we are not here by chance. Nobody is. We have this blanket of 'we are created equal,' but then we don't allow everybody to warm themselves. There's enough blanket."

Years later, she got to see her blood, sweat and tears pay off in a big way when she came to the set and watched me do my thing on *In Living Color*, at the time the hottest television show in the world. She even appeared in one of the sketches. I couldn't have been happier.

When Granny passed away on October 23, 2004, just four months before I won the Oscar for *Ray*, it was the close of an incredible American story. She got to see me rise to the highest heights. And she knew it all came about because of the hours and the toil she put in. That's what every parent wants to see— our children soar.

When I won the Academy Award, I paid tribute to her in my acceptance speech.

"She was my first acting teacher," I said from the stage. "She told me 'Stand up straight, put your shoulders back, act like you got some sense.'...She still talks to me, only now she talks to me in my dreams."

She didn't see me hold that statue in my hand, but she always knew I was destined for greatness. Even when I didn't know it myself.

There's not really a neat way to wrap up who Granny was as a person. It couldn't be done in a chapter for a book, it would at the very least need to be a series of books plus a podcast series to try to come close to capturing her. And even that wouldn't be enough. You just needed to know her. I'm lucky I did, and many of these stories play in my head like sitcom reruns, reminding me of where I learned about toughness and discipline and love.

When I am deep in the weeds, trying to figure out how to parent my daughters, it is the voice of my grandmother I hear, encouraging me, and of course yelling at me when I'm messing up as a parent. Thanks to her, I knew that it wasn't about always being your kids' best friend but being a parent. Even when it means you gotta be tough with them. Sometimes you gotta be tough *because* you love them. Just like she always loved me.

Though I guess I'm doing things a little bit differently, since I ain't trying to kill their joy.

YOU BETTER RECOGNIZE

B ecause I've had two children without being married to their mothers, the subject of marriage has hovered over my head in one way or another for years. Everyone's been asking me about getting married—my daughter's mothers, people in my family, strangers on the street, even Oprah (we'll get to her). I've just never been convinced that marriage was a good idea for me. I've had friends that have great marriages, others not so much. And it never seemed like marriage was necessary to raise my children in a safe and loving atmosphere. I just don't think I'm the marrying type. At least not for now—maybe in a few decades when I'm in a wheelchair and need somebody to push me around and change my diaper.

When I first met Connie in the early 1990s, I wasn't exactly at the top of the Hollywood game. If my career was Monopoly, I was far from owning Boardwalk. I didn't even own Baltic. I just kept landing on Chance cards that read, "Sorry, the casting director decided to go with Martin Lawrence."

I had decided to leave United States International University, the college I was attending at the time, to try my hand at show business, and I was hustling nonstop. Being a parent was still far from my mind. I was twenty-six and could spend my time as I wished, with no one to answer to and no real responsibilities. I had no idea how good I had it. As an up-and-coming comedian, the night time was the right time because that's when the comedy scene gets to poppin', and I used to hit three or four clubs on any given night, getting small glimpses of what the limelight was like— when you're onstage, you've got everybody's attention. But during the day, I worked at Thom McAn in the Fox Hills Mall and I only had the attention of broke-ass women and their badass kids. If you don't remember Thom McAn, this was not the place where the fly girls were going to buy their shoes.

"These shoes are plastic!" they would say to me after they came in the store by mistake.

"Yeah, but you can get ten of these motherfuckers for the one pair you trying to get down there at the high-end store," I'd answer.

More times than not, they would slip back in the store at closing time. The cheap shoes had been calling out to them. "Um, let me take a look at those shoes again."

"Yeah, I got you, girl."

When I wasn't hustling, you could find me down at Venice Beach, where, for the first time in my life, I wasn't the weirdest person around. It was a great spot to get material for comedy, from street comics slinging jokes to the basketball courts, where they played by prison rules. The only rule was there were no rules. You didn't call foul: You got popped in the mouth, you picked up your teeth and kept playing.

Then came *In Living Color*. If you were born very recently or lived in a cave during the early '90s, you might not know that when *In Living Color* came on TV it was an instant, motherfucking, monster hit, particularly in the Black community. When I first saw Damon and Keenan Ivory Wayans do that Mo' Money sketch, I was like, "What the fuck?!" "I'm Whiz, this is the Iceman!" "Chillin'!" I damn near laughed my Black ass off. And I was like, *How the hell do I get on that show?* My chance came when they were looking to add comedians to the cast after the second season and my manager threw me into the mix.

They started out with a hundred comedians—and I'm using the term "comedians" broadly. Some were jugglers, some did magic tricks, some were clowns. For real. Dressed up, head to toe, scarier than they were funny. I was stressed out of my mind and they kept whittling the people down and down and down until it was just me, Yvette Wilson, Steve Park and two others. The five of us had to go onstage for one final audition and perform in front of the entire cast. I showed up late on purpose, because I wanted to go last. By the way, I don't always recommend this tactic. A buddy of mine got fired because he showed up late on purpose. I told him, "Motherfucker, showing up late doesn't fly when you work at Jiffy Lube!"

I can't tell you how intimidating that final audition was. In my opinion, I was the funniest person on the planet...until I met the cast of *In Living Color*. Imagine performing in front of Jim Carrey, David Alan Grier, Keenen Ivory Wayans. Even the Fly Girls were there! That's actually where Jennifer Lopez got her start (on the same episode where I debuted).

But out of the five, I was the only one who actually did stand-up, so I definitely had an advantage. I killed it. I did a lot of characters back then. Most I can't remember, but I most definitely did my iconic character Wanda, and I think that's how I clinched the deal. I got a standing ovation from the house. And in the parlance of Hollywood, that's how I "got on."

One day back on the beach, I stumbled upon a pretty girl with short hair, wearing a red-white-and-blue bikini, gliding around on roller skates. I decided to approach and get that phone number. I didn't have much money, but I did have confidence. In the Hollywood business, you gotta fake it 'til you make it, and let's just say I was faking the funk. What does that mean? Little white lies. "My Benz is in the shop." "This is where I'm staying temporarily while my penthouse is being renovated." Bullshit like that.

So I was Mr. Thom McAn—broke and not fly, but faking it—when I approached the American flag bikini. I found out her name was Connie and she was twenty-four. When she gave me her phone number, I had to memorize it because I didn't have a pen to write it down. (Almost thirty years later, I still remember it.) What I loved about Connie was how cool and laid back she was. She worked in finance and had been in the air force. She was real grounded and had no interest in the limelight at all. Turned out, I didn't even need to front! She just liked me for me. And before I knew it, I had a girl and now all I needed was a bigger break.

Connie was by my side as I rose from obscurity. She was the ideal person to accompany me on the ride because she's such an even-keeled Capricorn—the same sign as my mom (you could write your own joke here). She was a perfect balance for me at the time to keep me humble. With my personality, I'd be trying to take up all the space; I'm the goofy comic, the guy with the lampshade on his head. That wasn't Connie at all. So sometimes, while driving her, I would slow down near a classy restaurant, roll down the windows and blast rap as loud as I could, staring down anyone who'd look over. I'd do it just to get a laugh outta Connie. She was incredibly embarrassed by it but I knew she secretly loved it.

All the fun and games came to a quick halt when we found out we were having a baby. Things got real in a hurry. Now I was twenty-six, she was twenty-four, but we were Hollywood young. If I was twenty-six in Texas in 1993, I would have been expected to be married and settled down already. Would already have five kids—two of them would have kids themselves. But Hollywood moved by a different clock. At least for men. Rick James didn't get his first hit until he was thirty. Jerry Seinfeld's TV show didn't happen until he was in his mid-thirties. So me at twenty-six, that's still Hollywood young.

My career was just taking off, I was off to the races and *BOOM*, life hits me right between the eyes. Connie told me she was pregnant and I remember my body filling with joy and fear at the same time. I didn't know how to be a father, I was still a kid myself! How was I supposed to change diapers in the middle of the night when I was still out in the comedy club? The most important thing to me was learning the latest dance moves. Not to mention my circumstances weren't traditional. I wasn't married. Connie and I already had problems in the relationship like any couple, so adding a pregnancy on top of that didn't help! Things got so stressful and tense that we stopped talking to each other halfway through the pregnancy. But after I simmered down, I realized that by not speaking with her I had left this woman to go through this intense experience all by herself. That bothered the shit out of me.

About two months before my daughter was born, when I was driving through Laurel Canyon, I thought seriously about where I was with all of this. My grandmother would have been really upset with me if she knew what I was doing. She knew she was about to be a great-grandmother but she didn't know I wasn't being there for Connie. She had always taught me that whatever the situation, it was important for me to step up and be a man. I remember her saying "Son, you made your bed, now you gotta sleep in it." I never fully understood that. If you were a furniture maker and you made beds for a living, you didn't have to sleep in each one. In fact, you could just buy a bed you didn't make yourself. But somehow, her words resonated with me and I knew I had to man up. If you did it, then you have to stay in it and be responsible. Not to mention, the closer the due date was, the more excited I was to have a baby girl. I was actually bringing someone into this world.

I called Connie on the phone. "Listen, I don't care, we may agree or disagree, not understand each other, but the thing is, we are having a baby. It's the best thing in the world. Let's do this the right way."

Connie and I talked it out and I pledged to be there for her. Those last two months were really important for our relationship, establishing a dynamic that continues to this day, more than twenty-five years later. Yeah, we still give each other a lot of shit, but we will always have each other's back.

So that covers Corinne's mother—next came Anelise's. Jumping ahead to 2000, I took a trip with a bunch of friends to Lake Havasu in Arizona, a wild party spot that had acquired the nickname Lake Have-a-Screw—which tells you everything you need to know about the place. In the midst of the craziness, I spotted an extremely sexy young lady wearing a "distinctive" teal-green bikini (why do I always keep noticing the bikinis first?!). Her name was Kristin and she was hard to miss. And while she was very pleasing to the eye, she also had a quiet, dignified air about her that distinguished her from the foolishness. I started talking to her and we hit it off.

The first night we hung out I actually cooked

for her, my special omelets. I'm not going to give away my secret recipe, but I'm a Southern boy from Texas, and you know everything is bigger in Texas—so my omelets have extra cheese, extra shrimp. You ain't lived 'til you've tried the Jamie Foxx shrimp and grits omelet. I guess Kristin liked them, because just a few months later she moved out to California.

When Kristin moved to Los Angeles, it allowed us to spend more time together. I was going through this career evolution and I was able to show her what was going on behind the Hollywood curtain—funny stories of trying to get parts, sharing my excitement and my frustration.

I was thirty-two and at a pivotal place in my career when we got serious. *The Jamie Foxx Show* was winding down and *Any Given Sunday*, a football movie I had filmed with Oliver Stone, had just been released. I didn't realize it at the time, but the arc of my career was about to change dramatically—I was about to go from a TV guy, a sitcom funnyman, to a dramatic movie star.

I was so happy in my relationship with Kristin but still wasn't changing my stance on marriage, even though our beautiful relationship brought Anelise into my life. I saw so many marriages collapsing around me. I was trying to stay away from that trauma. That didn't stop the questions from flying at me. When Oprah Winfrey asked me on her show if I was going to get married, I turned it back around on her.

"Oprah, are you married?"

"This is not about me, Jamie," Oprah said with a smile.

Oh, I see how it is, Oprah. You ask all the questions but I can't get just one in?!

My grandmother taught me that even if I wasn't married, I had to be a gentleman and take care of mine. You can still be a gentleman and not be married. Hold up, Grandma, so what you're saying is not only do I have to sleep in my own bed that I made, but I have to make other people's beds?! I get lost in metaphors but I get what she was saying.

Corinne later told me that when she was young, she wanted me and her mother to be married. Then she started seeing all of her friends' parents getting divorced by the time she got to high school and she saw how it wrecked them.

But if you're not married, people will often challenge you on your credibility, talking about love. It can be acquaintances, strangers, even my daughter Corinne. This happened on a trip we took to Paris. She was about seventeen and she wanted to bring along the guy who was her boyfriend at the time. She and I had gone the year before, just the two of us, but now she wanted to go to this romantic city with her high school sweetheart. I was like, "Oh, okay, I'm not enough for you, huh?" I put us up in three separate rooms in a fancy hotel, and I tried to give them some space to move around the city and see the wonderful sights.

The plan was for them to do the Louvre together, then I would pick them up and we all would go to Notre-Dame. When I came down to get in the car, I was stunned to see Corinne sitting in the back, crying. By herself.

"You okay?" I asked her. Usually, when someone is crying, they're clearly not okay. But you still ask.

"Dad, you promise not to get mad?" she said, between sobs.

"I don't promise nothing," I said. "I don't promise a motherfucking thing. What's up?"

"We had an argument," she said. "We were at the Louvre and I was trying to take a picture by a statue. He didn't want to wait on me—and he just left me."

While she was talking, I was already on the phone with my travel agent. "Get this motherfucker on the next plane smoking," I said into the phone.

She looked at me with widened eyes. "Dad, what are you doing?!"

"I'm gonna get him out of here."

"Dad, you're ruining everything!"

"*I'm* ruining everything? This dude left you at the Louvre and it's my fault? Nahhh!"

I stepped out of the car and called my sister on the phone, thinking perhaps I needed a woman's perspective on this. Deidra always gave me good advice in dealing with my daughters. First piece of advice she gave me: Never call in the middle of the night. My bad, I forgot about the time zone. When I explained the situation to her and asked what I should do, she said, "You can't get involved. You have to let that shit play out."

"Nah, nah, fuck that!" I said. I could hardly contain myself, I was so upset. "Deidra, this dude left my daughter at the Louvre. Anything could've happened!"

"Relax," she told me.

I took several deep cleansing breaths, then I got back in the car with Corinne.

"Corinne, you have a guy who claims to love you but his actions aren't matching his words," I said. "He's got to be dedicated to you!"

And then she lowered the boom on me. She said, "Dad, what do you know? You got two different kids from two different women. What do you know about love? What do you know?! How are you gonna tell me about my relationship? You're ruining everything for me!"

Because she so rarely came at me like that, I was devastated. *Okay, Jamie Foxx, the guy who has always felt like he can fix anything by being gregarious and funny and light, what you got now?* Usually, if I'm bombing during stand-up, I just go to the piano and bust out a tune, but it wasn't gonna work here. Sometimes my family's reaction to me clowning to cover up pain or a tense moment was like, *Mother- fucker, stop all that shit. Stop being charismatic and trying to touch up the painting.* Sometimes you got to let the shit be wrong and not try to touch it up. I had to quickly take a step back and try to reset the computer. I had to ask myself, Where was this coming from? How long has she felt this way?

I paused. "Okay, Corinne, I accept that. I hear you," I said.

I turned around to look at her. "But let me tell you what I do know about love. Yeah, me and your mom didn't get married. Me and your mom wasn't the typical Hollywood thing that you see on TV or in rom-com films. We weren't that. But you can't think of one time when your mom or you called me and I didn't drop everything to make sure you were alright. At any time in your life, you've never had to want or ask for anything. I'm not saying it's perfect, but love is different. Real love means nothing is bigger than your needs. I'll drop anything to make sure you're happy, to make sure you good. And there are things that happened that you don't even know about that I've done to make sure you good and your mom good. I'm not tooting my own horn, but the other thing of it is this: The person that loves you—and it's real love—would not leave you at the Louvre. They would man up, whatever the conversation will be. We have our argument and then we come back, but I wouldn't leave my baby at the Louvre."

She was looking at me now in sort of a state of shock. This was probably one of the realest conversations we had ever had.

One of the things I've always loved about Corinne is that she doesn't hold on to things. After we had that exchange, she exhaled in relief.

I had been trying to call her boyfriend on his cell phone, but he wasn't answering. I also called a few friends of mine, giving them the opportunity to talk me out of killing him. He was still under my care and he was somebody else's child, so I knew I couldn't kill the motherfucker. But what he was not going to do was ignore me.

I went down to the front desk and I called his room from there.

"Bonjour, bonjour," I said when he answered the phone, pretending I had a French accent so he would stay on the line.

"Uh, hello?" he said.

"Hang the phone up on me again, motherfucker. The fuck wrong with you?!" I said. "Listen. I'mma let you live. But I want you to understand something. You're under my care. You and her.

Something happens to you, something happens to her in this city, and I'm not there? I got to explain it to your parents. And you know how I feel about my daughter!

"I really think you're a good guy. But these types of mistakes are uncalled for. You can't, no way. No matter what, I'm going to give you a moral lesson that you can use even if you don't see my daughter anymore. Whoever your next relationship is. You have to man up. At the end of the day, when you're at the Louvre and you're with the person that you're supposed to love, if you have an argument, it is what it is. But the real king is not going to leave his queen at the Louvre. This ain't just about my daughter—it has to do with every daughter that you'll ever meet and you'll ever date. Understand that, bro. You know me. I'm the easiest person to get along with. But when it comes to my daughter, I will not have it."

When I was done, he was very quiet. I like to think that Corinne, who has such a good head on her shoulders, always picks the best guys, but sometimes love blinds you. And unfortunately, sometimes because of who I am, some people would harbor a certain resentment when they dated her. Like needing to cut down a privileged girl in a way to prove their manhood. I'm not saying that's necessarily what was going on here, but I warned her that she needed to be careful about that. And I warned plenty of guys that came into her life that I may need to beat their ass if they wrong my baby girl.

I wanted her to understand what it felt like when a guy truly respected her—and what it felt like when he didn't. I had been trying to model that for years with Corinne's mother, all through our relationship ups and downs. Respect. In my mind, everything started there.

DAD RULE NO. 1:
YOU GOTTA SHOW UP

The reason why I try to throw so much love and understanding at my kids is because, although I had great adoptive parents, I still grew up with a real longing—sometimes conscious, sometimes subconscious—for my biological mother and father and their love. It's one thing to be adopted and not know who your parents are. You wonder who your dad is; he could be a random sperm donor that works at the post office or he could be a famous NBA star like Wilt Chamberlain—after all, he did claim to have slept with 20,000 women (which makes me wonder when he had time to play for the Lakers). But when you're adopted *and* you know who your biological parents are...it's like, "Hey, I'm right fucking here." It's like you're a used car that got sold and you see your previous owner taking the bus. You're telling me you'd rather ride in a bus that smells like piss than drive your own son? I'm mixing metaphors here, but I wanted to make sure that my children never felt like an abandoned Volvo.

My mother had such a hard time showing up for me. So did my father. Sometimes it would be the small things that would bother me, like being taken to and picked up from school. My mother never once did that. Neither did my father. When I was young, I tried to block it out, not think about it, minimize it. But as I got older, I looked back and saw that it did affect me. My dad, the person who brought me into the world, who is supposed to love me, who I'm supposed to talk to every day, wasn't around. He never even gave me the sex talk. I still managed to figure it out, but there was some trial and error involved. It wasn't like today where XXX adult content is just one click away. But that fucks up kids in a different way. Sidebar: Be sure to check your kids' internet history. They know that technology shit better than us.

So the person who is supposed to tell me how to be as a man—that person ended up being a stranger to me. In my early days in LA, sometimes it would weigh on me that I knew more about the people I became friends with than I did my own mother and father. The sadness of it all is that you can't get that time back.

Was I disappointed? Yes. Was I devastated to the point that I couldn't go on? Not quite. I think the only reason was because my grandmother and grandfather were always there to soften the abandonment blow.

When I did see my biological father, Darrell Bishop, I would wind up frustrated by my failure to connect with him. By the time I was born he had converted to the Nation of Islam and changed his name to Shahid Abdullah. The story I'm told is that he was trying to make me observe the Ramadan fast when I was just seven months old and my grandmother got concerned that he and my mother were endangering my health. That was one of the reasons she prevailed upon my mother to give me up for adoption, so she could raise me properly.

My father was so close to his religion; I couldn't fault a man for what he believed the afterlife would be. But while he strove to prepare himself for the afterlife, I wondered why he couldn't think more about being a father to his son here on earth.

One of my earliest memories is a conversation I observed between my father and my grandmother, when he was trying to explain to her that she needed to call him by his Muslim name.

"Darrell, it's good to see you," she said.

"Um, Mrs. Talley, I'm no longer Darrell," he said.

"Well, who are you?"

"Uh, I'm Shahid Abdullah. I'm a Muslim," he answered.

"Uh, well, Darrell, Sha-shit is what I say. This is a Baptist home, and you are going to go by Darrell Bishop. Now we ain't about that devil."

If it wasn't Baptist, my grandmother didn't want any part of it. This is the same woman who wouldn't even let me listen to a Prince record because she thought it was devil worship, so she was unlikely to go along with his name change. I guess her forward thinking only extended so far.

Growing up, I remember my father was very refined, reserved, well educated, good-looking—well, maybe not Billy Dee Williams good-looking, but good-looking enough to birth a Jamie Foxx (who I also find very handsome). Though he never made much money, I was told he was a talented singer who once performed for the Queen of England, but I never heard him sing. At least he would try to feign interest in the things I was doing. He came to watch me play football once in a while, and he'd say, "You scored a touchdown. That's fantastic!" He said "fantastic" a lot. Then he'd ask me questions I didn't quite understand.

"So, when you're doing those touchdowns, how do you feel?"

"I don't know, man. I just scored a touchdown."

"Wow, fantastic! The Honorable Elijah Muhammad says…"

That was the prelude to every sentence, quoting the Honorable Elijah Muhammad. I would often get frustrated talking to him, not understanding why we couldn't connect.

"Dad, why don't me and you go out and—"

"Hey, well, the Honorable Elijah Muhammad said…"

I wanted to tell him, "Darrell—correction, Shahid—I don't really understand all of that. I just want to have a connection." I was sixteen, a star quarterback in Texas, where football is literally worshipped. I was a baller, I wasn't a bad kid, I had two jobs, everybody loved me. "So why are you not here for every game, cheering me on?"

"Well, the Honorable Elijah—"

Whoever this "honorable" dude was, all I knew was that he was standing between me and my father.

When I became a dad, I still didn't know a lot about the Honorable Elijah, but I knew all about the Benjamins—and I knew I didn't have any. The reality of my financial situation was such a huge issue for me that I wasn't thinking straight. Even though I was one of the stars of a hit show, *In Living Color*, I was running out of money.

In Living Color paid about six grand a week, but we

only worked six weeks at a time, once a year, to film a whole season. The bills were piling up. Even though we were no longer together, I was trying to pay for my place and also a place for Corinne and her mom. Things were extremely strained. Hopefully, Corinne wasn't aware of how bad it was. All she knew was every week I was flying to places like Poughkeepsie and Maine and Vermont to do shows.

I played everything close to the vest, the way I saw my grandfather do as I was growing up. He never let it show when the money was dwindling. I knew we didn't have a lot, but they never let me go hungry. We didn't have the best food, like the name brands I saw in the commercials. I didn't get Hostess brand Ding Dongs, I had off-brand Ping Pongs. Not as good and just as unhealthy. The Little Debbie on the snacks I ate had a mustache. But I always knew when I opened the cupboard or the fridge there would be something there. My grandfather passed away at eighty, when I was in LA. As we made the funeral preparations, I checked his billfold: He had just two dollars in his pocket. But he didn't live as a poor man.

When Corinne was little, I definitely had days when I went to the ATM and couldn't withdraw any money because I didn't have enough to get twenty bucks. Brother was busted. Even if it might have been the wrong approach, I felt like I had to be a

superhero in the eyes of Corinne. I couldn't let them
see me with my cape off. I think part of the job of
Dad, even if it might sound like wrong-headed man
code, is you don't let the family know everything
that's going on, because we gotta keep up family
morale. We must go out there and bring the fresh kill
home. That's just how it was when I was growing up:
Men didn't cry. Even in *Glory*, Denzel was a slave,
he got whipped by Ferris Bueller and still—he only
hit you with the one single tear. Y'all remember that
shit? Denzel was a beast (another actor with slightly
more Oscars than me, but I'm catching up).

But as the times changed and I changed, I learned
that part of being a man is to show vulnerability
and that it's okay to let your family in. Just as much
as I wanna help them when they're struggling, they
wanna help me when I'm struggling. And as I've
gotten older, I've become more emotional. I'll cry
at the drop of a hat, and I'm not talking about a
little sniveling cry—I'm talking about the full-blown
Viola Davis cry, with the snot and all.

The irony is little Corinne didn't care what I
was trying to do or how much I had in my bank
account. It was no different than how I felt when
I was little, when I just yearned for my parents to
show up. The only thing that mattered to her was
that I walked through those doors when it was her
special day with Dad, but I didn't yet see that it

was the cycle repeating itself. I didn't get those days right all the time, whether because I was working or maybe I just dropped the ball. I did try to make up for the times when I fumbled—though I found out later that didn't work as well as I thought it did at the time. I missed that recital? Well, then, how about we go to Disneyland for two days in a row. I used Mickey Mouse as an emotional Band-Aid, as if he could do my bidding for me. You want some more cotton candy, Corinne? We can get free churros from Mickey because of who I am—isn't that great, Corinne?

It all came back to bite me in the ass years later when we went to a family therapist and she said she just wanted me present. It was during that session, when Corinne was fifteen, that I found out Corinne hated me.

Okay, maybe she didn't use the word "hate"— but in my mind she might as well have. I wasn't crazy about the idea of spilling my guts on some professional's couch. I knew we were having some challenges with communication. For example, when I told Corinne she wasn't allowed to be dating until she was thirty, she thought I was using hyperbole. But I was dead-ass serious. I did finally lighten up and agree on twenty-eight. Then she brought up I was twenty-six when I had her—what can I say? She was always a good math student.

But I thought communication breakdowns were just part of the deal when you're raising teenage girls. When my old-school I'm-your-daddy-and-you're-the-daughter type of bossy approach failed to connect with Corinne, she suggested we try therapy. I was like, "Huh?" #BlackPeopleDontGoToTherapy.

But she was confiding in her mom and not telling me anything. Like too many dads, I wasn't listening to her when she tried to talk to me, instead giving her my opinion about what she should be doing. I think my fame also got in the way. I didn't realize how much she hated the glitz and superficiality of Hollywood. But I soon found out. I guess Corinne was right; we needed some help. I didn't realize how much she hated what came along with what I do for a living.

When we got into it at the therapist's office, it was like watching a movie scene where you hear a rewinding sound effect and they do a flashback, showing you what actually happened—now told through the perspective of the daughter instead of the father. I got Corinne's version of her childhood.

(Rewind) "Remember that time when we were in Miami?" she said.

"Oh yeah, you had a great time, didn't you?"

She rolled her eyes. "Actually, you went out a lot and somebody else watched me. Where were you, Dad? And you would hang out late and wake up late, so I would miss the beach. We really went there for you, not for me."

Ouch.

"But you gotta understand, Corinne. It was a promotional trip and—"

"Let her talk," the therapist said, interrupting me.

"No, but I—"

"Let her talk," the therapist repeated.

"And then there were the girls that were around," Corinne said.

"What girls?" I said. "There were no girls around."

"Daaaad. There were girls all the time."

"But that was my friend," I said.

"Dad. It was girls all the time," she said. "It was girls. It was parties. I saw it all."

"Um, but what about Disneyland?" I said, trying to find something to save me.

"I could really give a fuck about Mickey Mouse," she responded.

And then she looked at the therapist and said, "I just didn't love my dad that much."

I think I might have blacked out for a second when I heard that sentence. I was devastated. I started thinking back to all the occasions when I thought I was Super Dad because I was bringing her to all these places. I realized I was just tricking myself, making myself feel good. *Oh, you're Super Dad because you took her to Miami.* But what probably would have been more valuable was to just have more simple, quiet moments when it was just me and her. There was no way to dance around the emotional deficit that I had caused by thinking my financial commitment to her was enough. I was blindsided—but I was so grateful she told me how she was feeling. I still had time to fix it.

Even though she went to school with other celebrity kids, Corinne wasn't interested in glamour and limelight. What interested her was connecting with people, not impressing people. She started the cheerleading squad at her high school when she realized there was no squad to cheer on the football and basketball teams. That's who Corinne was.

"Dad, I like simple stuff," she told me. "I like steak and potatoes—do you realize that? You're always taking me to Mr. Chow's."

"But baby, they got that special chicken with peanut sauce." (That peanut sauce is really next level.)

Even though the therapy session was not fun for me, I felt like she deserved to have that. She deserved to have the chance to cuss her dad out because she had been so sweet and considerate for so many years. She had never gotten in trouble, had never caused us any angst. She always came home when she was supposed to, never got pregnant, did drugs, or brought home some idiot. I used to say, "Corinne, you ever gonna fuck up? Because I got all these parent-type things I want to say, like 'Don't you ever bring your goddamn ass in this motherfucking house this late.' I never got a chance to say that. 'Is this drugs?!' I never got a chance to say none of that!"

And, back to the therapy session. Maybe her dad deserved to get cussed out a little. Even though, traditionally, Black parents don't play that shit. But sometimes, Black or not, you need to hear the truth.

When I decided that the answer to my money problems was to move from LA to Las Vegas when Corinne was young, I kind of lost sight of what it might do to Corinne. But you gotta look at it from my perspective: I was living large on two acres of land, copped a mansion for $280,000, I was living life like a rock star, every night on the Strip, everybody knew my name. Even now, I'm getting caught up just thinking about it. But if I could go back in time, I'd check my dumb ass. I buried how painful it was when my parents seemed to forget about me, and here I was, caught up and repeating the cycle.

But once the novelty of Vegas ended, a problem I faced was that I immediately felt like I was out of the loop. Not only was I out of money, I also was running out of artistic steam. Out of work. Out of cash. And out of sight of my daughter, who I truly missed. My manager knew I was desperate to get back to LA. We had started shopping a sitcom called *The Jamie Foxx Show* that would be a starring vehicle for me. We were getting a lot of noes. In Hollywood, once you've been on a hit show, people look at you like you already had your turn. I had done *In Living Color*. My turn was over. But I wasn't done. I ain't dead yet. I ain't even thirty yet! What was I supposed to do? Start a new career? Somehow, I don't feel like I'd be a good waiter. Because if you said the wrong shit to me, I would most definitely be spitting in your food. And if you don't tip me right, I'm meeting you in the parking lot.

But I knew I had the talent and I had a great idea. Sometimes it's just a matter of the fit. Warner Bros., at the time the WB, was badly in need of new shows that could take off. My manager asked me what I thought.

"What do you think?" he asked me. "We've taken *The Jamie Foxx Show* to all these other different places. How do you feel about the WB?"

"I like the people that like me," I said. "If Warner Bros. likes me, let's go there." Best of all, the show would get me back to LA.

When *The Jamie Foxx Show* aired, it killed in the ratings, doing Seinfeld-type numbers. But in terms of my parenting, the show was a blessing and a curse. The blessing was money was now coming in. I could take care of things, both for myself and for my daughter. The curse? The nonstop partying.

Sometimes I would go too far with it. I called myself a responsible dad, though I admit my self-awareness might have been a little cloudy. A little fucked up. For example, there was this one trip to Miami. My friend suggested we go to a huge party that was happening that night. Aaannd, yeah, you can probably see where this is going. The party overlapped with the time I was supposed to be with my daughter. When I finally caught up with her, I did everything I could to make sure she had a fun day—I took her to the pool, then the beach, then the pool, then the beach, then the pool. This wasn't one of those Miami trips she'd complain about later. But I wasn't myself.

"Corinne, let's go to the beach!"

"Hey, Corinne, let's go to the pool!"

Until I wore her out trying to overcompensate. I made sure after that day that I never did that again; I would never let partying get in the way of hanging with my little girl.

That was until the next time…when I was in Miami on a later trip, I decided I wanted Corinne, now six, to come see me. I was kicking it with my homies, but I knew my daughter was flying in. I announced to everyone, "Listen, I have to go to bed so I can grab my daughter in the morning."

But I didn't go to bed. We partied all night. I had the driver take me straight from the club to the airport. But I didn't have my ID. When I headed to the terminal, I didn't think I would have any problems. I wasn't yet JAMIE FOXX all caps—I was still Jamie Foxx lowercase. But I had acquired a bit of celebrity. I had my share of fans. I had my TV show, but I realized on that day not everybody watched the WB.

I thought I'd stroll in, retrieve my daughter and we'd be on our way. However, when I got there, with Corinne just a few feet away from me, I was not allowed access to her. This isn't my daughter's fault. All she wants to do is run into her father's arms; instead, there I was, arguing with the flight attendants and local authorities, asking them, "Please, let me have my daughter."

As we bickered back and forth, a few patrons came up and said, "Aren't you that guy on that show?"

"Yes, yes, I'll sign anybody's autograph!" I said, grateful for the opportunity to show these people who I was.

Even though I signed the autographs, it appeared I was going to be unsuccessful. Until finally, one more autograph request, from an airport employee they knew and respected, moved them to change their mind and let me have Corinne. My six-year-old daughter had never seen any of my television shows, so she wasn't impressed with my efforts to get around the rules. She stood there, a few feet away, with a scowl on her face. Her lips were curled in that expression

I've come to recognize on every Black woman I know. The look is usually accompanied by two words: "This muthafucka." Corinne had the look, but maybe not the words yet. She suggested to me that one of two things needed to happen.

"Dad, either you should never forget your ID—or you need to do bigger shows."

Perfect comic timing at age six. *That's my girl.*

In Miami, Corinne stayed with me at the Delano hotel. Any trip to Miami was really for my pleasure, but I told myself that I was being a good father by having Corinne with me. In retrospect, it probably wasn't a whole lot of fun for a kid—but I was making myself feel good. I was faking myself out. I know I've said that the most important thing is being there for your kid—but it doesn't end there. You still gotta connect with them. Even when my dad *was* around, he wasn't always present with me. And I wasn't as present with Corinne as I should've been.

But Corinne was usually willing to give me a pass. I guess she could see I was trying—even if it didn't always go to plan. One time, we were sitting at the Delano pool in Miami Beach and I slowly began to realize something was wrong with this picture. The water was clear, we had bottle service, the women were topless...Oh shit! Topless?! *Fuck!* I shouted in my head. Corinne sat there at the edge of the pool, playing with a toy.

"Corinne, I want to tell you something," I said. She looked up at me, waiting. "The pool is, um…"

"I know, Dad, it's topless," she said.

"What?"

"Yeah, Dad, I know it's topless," she repeated. "And one of those ladies doesn't look good at all." She went back to her toy.

She could have given me a hard time, even at age six, but she didn't. It was a powerful lesson for me, one I think that's instructive for all fathers. If they see you trying, they're usually going to give you somewhat of a break. That means it's never too late to try. After my mother remarried, to a man named George Dixon, they had two daughters, Deidra and DeOndra. When my stepfather's relationship with Deidra fell on hard times, I saw him give up, thinking it was too late to repair things when they were both adults—too much time had passed. But that was a mistake. You can't give up. There are going to be times when you take a loss, and it's going to be painful. To use a sports analogy, you're going to be down by five, then you're going to be down by fifteen and then twenty. In that situation it might seem fruitless to put five points up on the board—too little too late. But when it comes to your kids, you have to keep putting points on the board. It's never fruitless.

It was indescribable how terrific I'd feel when I

walked into a room after I had been away for a while and she screeched "Daddy!" and ran up and hugged my leg. *Oh wow, she still digs me! I'm still okay.* It would bring tears to my eyes. I've also got to give her mother credit for not bad-mouthing me for my frequent absences and letting me find my own way as a parent.

These joyous reunions with my daughter would sometimes make me cast my mind back to my own father and how seldom I had the opportunity to run up and hug him. Did he not long for such reunions? Didn't he yearn to see his child's love expressed so purely? How could he not feel that little jolt when he came around me and I was just so damn happy to see him? But even though I learned from my dad's parenting (or lack thereof), the reverse wasn't possible. I couldn't be like Corinne and give my dad a break for trying…because he *wasn't* trying. It just wasn't comparable.

And even though there was never a cathartic resolution with my dad, I did eventually let go of that anger and resentment. The lesson is you have to keep making an effort with your kids: You gotta show up, no matter what. But with other people in your life, sometimes it's just not worth it. Got no more time for hate.

THE SWITCH FROM THE SWITCH

The difference between how I was disciplined in the 1970s and '80s in Texas and how I discipline my daughter Anelise now is so enormous that it blows my mind. When I fucked up in Terrell, I knew as soon as my grandparents found out, it wouldn't take long before one of them said, "Boy, go out there and get that switch."

If you're over forty and you were raised in the South, you probably know what a switch is. For those of you who aren't or weren't, Webster's defines "switch" as "the ass-whupping part of a tree." But you can't be messing with the switch in 2021. If you go in the backyard to look at some trees, you better be bird-watching. If not, somebody is calling Child Protective Services on your ass.

But it never crossed my mind to whup my kids anyway. I knew I couldn't do things like Estelle and Mark even if I wanted to, and I needed a different approach to instilling discipline. One that wouldn't end with me in handcuffs. But typical LA punishments didn't fit my style as a parent either. "Go to your room!" Oh, where all their electronics are? That's where they wanna be! "Time-out!" What the hell is a time-out? When I was a kid, the only "time-out" I got was when my grandfather caught his breath between whupping that ass.

Instead, I used the specter of disappointing me as a method to keep them in line. For Anelise, one of the worst things that could happen to her is for me to give her a look telling her that she has let me down. Side note to parents: Practice this look in a mirror daily.

One day when I was spending time with Anelise and her mother, Anelise came into the room and asked me, "Dad, do you know this guy on TikTok?"

I wasn't too sure what TikTok was, but the hackles started rising on the back of my neck. Why the hell would somebody be contacting my adolescent daughter on PlikPlok or whatever the hell it is? Now I'm suspicious. She showed me the guy on her phone.

"Nah, I don't know that motherfucker," I said. Yeah, I don't sugarcoat my language for Anelise. I think it's important for her to get the unadulterated, real version of Dad. Kill me.

"Well, he DMed me and said he knew you, so I figured he's one of your friends, so I started talking to him," she said. My friend? The only DMing my friends do is drink martinis, with fly honeys around.

Anelise saw the expression that came over my face—probably the equivalent of the bulging-eyes emoji. In other words, Dad was about to lose his shit. It was a shocked expression she had never seen before, and it dawned on her that she had done something wrong. Her face collapsed. Written all over it were the words, *Damn, I fucked up, huh?*

"We gotta talk," I said. She grimaced like she was about to take cough medicine.

"What is it?" I asked.

"I hate it when you say we gotta talk."

"Why?"

"I can't take it," she said, moaning. "I can't take it. I can't take it."

In that instance, it wasn't even necessary for me to raise my voice. She knew she had messed up.

Anelise doesn't mess up very often, so when she does it becomes headline news. Her mother was there with me, so we got to do good cop, bad cop—with me as the bad cop, which is great for me because the villain is always more fun to play (especially when I get to kick Spider-Man's ass). To teach her the lesson I wanted to get across in that moment, I knew I had to immediately get her attention, and I knew that had to be through who she really looked up to—her older sister, Corinne.

Corinne was an only child until she was fourteen. Then, in the same year, her mother had a daughter and I had Anelise. And because she was so much older than her half sisters, her maternal instinct kicked in. I think one reason Anelise really connects with Corinne is because Anelise has always been an introvert. I, on the other hand (believe it or not) have always been an extreme extrovert. So Corinne was there for Anelise to let her know it's okay to be quieter and more thoughtful and not wild and crazy like Daddy. Anelise really connected with Corinne, so I knew if this was a Corinne story, Anelise would be all ears.

When Corinne first got on Instagram, she was about seventeen or eighteen. The social media explosion was just starting. Like most dads, I was not totally up to speed on what she was doing on her phone, so I got blindsided when this went down. The internet was the Wild West! First you started getting floppy disks in the mail for AOL, then you got email, then you realized *Oh shit, there's titties here!* People can do whatever they want on here and that's fun...until you're a dad. And then it gets scary. People can do whatever they want on here...to your kids. And that ain't cool.

Corinne put up a post on Instagram that showed her location, and she talked about what she was doing at the mall. The next thing you know, some dude showed up out of nowhere. She called me on the phone, alarmed.

"Who the fuck is he? And what is he doing here?!" I asked her.

"Well, Dad, I think it's because I said I was at the mall."

"You said what?!"

It got to the point where this sick guy started stalking Corinne, harassing her online and sometimes in person. It was really serious; I was in a constant state of rage and panic. I had to get my people on it, to find out who this guy was. I got a full rundown—where he lived, what his history was. We had to keep tabs on him to see how he was moving. The guy turned out to be a Black dude, an ex-Marine in his late twenties who was armed and dangerous.

When I told this to Anelise, she gasped.

"Yeah, the motherfucker was crazy. He was saying, 'I'm gonna kill you.' It had something to do with God and God's children."

Anelise was apoplectic. She sat there in shock, wondering if she had just invited Satan into our lives.

"First of all, breathe," I told her. "It's gonna be okay. But these are things you need to know. You can't just open that door for people without being very, very cautious. You're eleven years old. I need to be careful of everything that happens with you.

"Of course the dude is gonna say he knows me," I said. "You know why? Because that's all the internet does. People prop themselves up or they lie to make sure they look good on the internet. If you would have asked him, 'Do you know Martin Luther King?' he would've said, 'Yeah, I was with that nigga yesterday, it was crazy.' You could have asked him anything. 'You know Muhammad Ali?' 'Yeah, it was crazy, I was sparring with that nigga last week.'"

But she needed to know that her actions have consequences. And better that those consequences come from me than some stranger. I had to shut some stuff down.

"I'm taking your phone away for now, Anelise," I said. And then I remembered she had way more shit. So I took the iPad, the iPod, the iMac, even her iToaster. She was forced to use the regular toaster in the kitchen without text messaging capabilities.

Back in Texas, I didn't have shit that got taken away because I didn't have shit at all. The lessons I got there came to me with a different kind of spice on them. Especially when the lesson came from my grandfather, who I called "Edaddy." He spoke softly but carried a big stick—especially when it came to good old-fashioned Southern whuppings. Back when getting your fanny blasted was still acceptable, he was the Michael Jordan of the strap. Just picture a trophy like the Heisman with his likeness, strap in hand, ready to whup ass. I don't know exactly how many times I got whupped, but I know that it was enough for a lifetime.

One whupping that always stands out to me happened when I was in the fifth grade, hanging out with my friend Kyle. The streetlights were about to come on and my grandparents had a rule—when the streetlights are about to come on, you have your ass in the house. But Kyle seemed to think everything was cool. I don't know if his house had different rules or maybe that's just how it was when you're white. I watched Kyle go in his house and talk to his mom.

"You know it's late, Kyle," she said very nicely.

He said, "Whatever, Mom. Get off my back! Where's dinner?"

Wow. Kyle's pretty brave, I thought. So, when I got back to my house on the southside, my grandmother met me at the door with "Boy, you done lost your goddamn mind. You see the streetlights is on!" But since I was feeling white, I channeled Kyle and said, "Whatever, Granny, get off my back. Where's dinner?"

As soon as the words left my mouth, I knew I had fucked up. My grandmother got so mad that I would have sworn her head spun around like that little girl in the movie *The Exorcist*.

"Oh, you been hanging out with your little white friend, huh?" she said. "You think you white? Well, your little white friend gonna get your ass tore up tonight. Wait until your grandfather gets home!"

I was still feeling myself. Clearly my senses had headed for the exits. I responded, "Whatever!" And then I went to my room. But when I said "Whatever," I didn't say it quite as confidently, because I knew when she turned it over to the godfather of the belt, shit was about to get dark.

There I was, sitting in my room, contemplating my fate. It was no use trying to find something to distract me; it wouldn't have worked. I just waited. My senses not only came back, they went on high alert. I heard extra clear when that Chevrolet truck pulled up into the driveway. I could hear the car door open with a creak and close with a thud. Those brogan boots hit the concrete with heavy footfalls. The fence opened with a squeak. He walked into the house and quickly my grandmother filled him in on my nonsense. The high female voice, followed by a low, male "Mm-hmm." Back and forth. Then he got louder.

"Bring your ass, boy! Come on and get it!"

I lost thirty pounds when I heard his voice. I tried

to summon as much manhood as I could as I walked in to face my fate. The belt strap had already been taken off like he was a gunslinger in a John Wayne movie. He grabbed me by my neck and clamped his legs down over my head. You would have thought he was in the Kentucky Derby coming into the last turn. But I had a plan—I was gonna twist out of it. Escape. But really all I did was twist my body so that I was now facing him while he whipped. His legs still had me clamped. As he continued to bring down the fury, it wasn't just the strap heating me up now. My grandfather dipped snuff, so he had Levi Garrett in his mouth at all times. While he was whipping my behind, the juice was flying out of his mouth—and landing in my eyes, my mouth, all over my face. I was disgusted and horrified, but all I could do was swallow it and pray it would be over soon. It was a night I'll remember forever. After that, whenever I saw any light—streetlight, flashlight, car light—I'd break into a sweat and make like Spike Lee: Do the right thing.

My second most memorable whupping came four years later, when I was fourteen and decided that instead of going to my piano lessons, I would attend Six Flags with my friends. Just reading back this sentence now, "instead of going to my piano lessons, I would attend Six Flags," I cannot believe the audacity I had to think I might get away with that. What can I say? I was a pretty confident kid. Maybe a little too confident.

Piano lessons were great for me, but they were also a monkey wrench in my social life. Every weekend I would travel from Terrell to Dallas to take my piano lesson, but I would've rather spent the weekends hanging out with friends. Every single summer, when school ended, all the kids planned a trip to Six Flags. All they'd talk about was the Big Bend, the Fiesta Train, all sorts of wild rides. I pictured a full day of freedom, running around acting crazy. Years had gone by and I never got a chance to go to Six Flags because of my piano lessons. I would've been happy to just check out Elmer Fudd's Fewwis Wheel! My friends would joke about it.

"Hey man, you think your grandma gonna let you hang out with the fellas and go to Six Flags or you gonna be a momma's boy, playing piano like a wannabe Stevie Wonder?"

First of all, I was more of a wannabe Ray. Second, I was a grown man and I told them I was going to Six Flags this year. They all laughed. "Yeah, good luck."

As the days led up to the trip, I worked out a plan. I already had my fly Six Flags outfit all picked out—my tan Members Only jacket, Calvin Klein jeans, Izod shirt and K-Swiss sneakers. Only one thing—I hadn't asked my grandparents yet. I was still building up the courage!

I had a request for my best friend, Gilbert. "Hey man, have your mother call my grandmother and see if she could work it out."

I listened to the one-sided call. "Hell naw!" Granny said as she hung up. She didn't say shit to me, almost daring me to ask her. I wanted to but I was scared. I knew my plans were looking dim. When Saturday came, my moment of truth, my grandfather came into the room as I stood there in my Six Flags outfit. He said the same thing he said every Saturday, "Come on, boy, we going to piano lessons."

Something in me churned. I felt like this was the moment for me to turn into a man. I mustered up every bit of courage I could, I looked him semi in his face and said, "I ain't going to piano lessons." In my mind I thought I delivered that clearly. But evidently I was so scared I mumbled it, because he said, "Boy, what you say?"

Although it started mumbly, it was exciting to stand up for myself. So I built up more courage, looked him square in the face and said, "You heard what I said. I'm not going to piano les—"

Pow! Before I could finish the sentence, I felt a burning sensation in my sternum. My grandfather had punched me square in the chest. I went flying backward and landed on the other side of the piano bench.

"Get your ass up!" he said, looking down at me.

When I finally dragged myself from under the piano, I realized I wasn't going to Six Flags. I was bummed I couldn't go have fun with my friends, I was humiliated that I didn't have (and even needed) permission from my grandparents. I felt like I didn't have any control, so I took the only control I could...and decided to run away.

I fled the house and ran around the corner to Southwestern Christian College, an HBCU where I spent a lot of my time hanging with the musicians on campus. I was only fourteen, but I had gotten to know some of the students because we sometimes played music together at church events. At this point Six Flags was beside the point. I was trying to make a statement, to exercise my independence. Or something. In reality, I didn't have anything resembling a plan. I stayed at the college for several hours. But then I started getting hungry.

I called one of my friends from a pay phone, a girl named Nina. Maybe she'd be able to help me figure out what to do. She was always the voice of reason—to me and everyone else. Whenever a fight broke out, she'd get in the middle and just ask questions about how you're feeling. And trying to explain why you're mad would often make you feel dumb and you'd stop being mad altogether.

"Where you at, boy?" she said. "Your grandmother

is going crazy looking for you. She crying. Go home. What're you doin' anyway? You know you just went around the corner."

"I'm a man," I said.

Nina laughed. "You ain't no man! Go home, boy. You silly."

"You think I should go home?"

"Go home!"

We had one of those blocks where you knew who was cooking by the smell that hit your nose. *Oh, Miss Scott is making chicken! Oooh, Miss Thomas making that casserole!* As soon as I turned onto my block, the wonderful fragrance from my grandmother's pork chops hit my nose. She cooked them in a batch of old grease. Once they hit the pan, it would make that beautiful sizzling sound. *Pffft.* She'd leave the screen door open so the kitchen wouldn't fill with smoke. As a result, the whole neighborhood could smell it. Everybody would be walking around rubbing their bellies.

Grandma was going all out on this evening. I could smell the pork chops, the cornbread, the whole nine. I was so hungry I thought I was gonna pass out. When I walked into the house, my stomach was wide open.

"Granny. You alright?" I asked.

"I'm fine," she said without looking at me. "I ain't been looking for you."

But I knew she had been. "Can I eat?"

"Well, it's food," she said. "If you want food."

We never talked any more about it. I knew I had hurt her. And even though my grandfather wasn't shy about tearing into my ass, it was seeing how I let down my grandmother that ended up stinging the most. I took that with me into fatherhood. Sure, beating your kids went out of fashion (probably for good reason), but you can still hit them with a disappointed look. And you don't have to be an Academy Award–winning actor (though it helps) to get them feeling guilty. So maybe I brought some Texas-style discipline with me to LA after all.

And, last but not least, I go to Six Flags now whenever the fuck I want. Goliath, Full Throttle, X2, fuck them piano lessons, I got a year pass to Magic Mountain.

SNITCHES GET STITCHES

In fifth grade, my grandmother showed me how much families were supposed to have each other's backs. It was about as memorable an example of this lesson as any bighead little boy could ever witness. I was at the house of my best friend, Bryan, when his older brother, Ed, came into the room playing with a pellet gun. Ed told Bryan—who went by the name "Kill D" (no, he didn't kill nobody...that I know of)—to hold the pellet gun on me.

"Ed, what's that mean?" I asked him. I already knew this meant trouble.

"Let's chest box," Ed responded. "But here's the deal. If you hit me in my chest, my brother is gonna shoot you with the pellet gun."

WTF? What kind of game is this? And why would I want to play it? It's lose-lose for me! But I also didn't seem to have a choice. I looked at Kill D, who was my age, and asked him, "You really gonna do this?" On top of being awful, this game didn't seem fair to me! I didn't have a brother pointing a pellet gun at no one.

He said, "Man, if it's between me killing you and my brother killing me, I got to kill you."

The chest boxing went horribly for me. I got hit in the chest—hard—and when I hit back, I almost got shot with the gun. I saw Kill D with the gun pointed at me and he was about to pull the trigger. But, thank the Lord, he put it down. Maybe he decided not to live up to his nickname at that point. But I really thought I could die, so I went back home and I sat outside my house, crying. Not that whimpering cry, but the wracking kind of cry where your chest is heaving and you can't get your words together. My grandmother overheard me and came outside. She was just inside but she could've overheard me from the supermarket.

"Boy, what's wrong with you? What the hell y'all doing?"

I said, in cry language, "Ed...(sob sob)...pellet gun...chest box...(sob sob)...shoot me...Ed."

"Ed did what?" she said.

"He tried to shoot me."

"Well, you hold on a second."

She went in the house and put on another muumuu. I guess it was her fighting muumuu. She came out and said, "You come with me."

There we were, walking down the street together, just like a scene out of *A Bronx Tale*. As she walked in front of me, I noticed the right side of her muumuu was swinging from left to right. What was that in her pocket? When we got to Ed's house, I discovered what it was. She reached into her pocket and pulled out the shiny .380 before she knocked on the front door. As I looked at the .380, a little gas bubbled up in my stomach. *What the hell is Granny 'bout to do?*

"Who is it?" said Ed's mother on the other side of the door. Her eyes widened when she opened the door and saw my grandmother's .380 staring back at her.

"Listen. I raised you and everybody in this city. But if I have to come back here again and talk to you about Ed, it's not gonna be good."

Granny looked into the house, where she saw Ed standing. Ed looked like a deer caught in headlights—if the headlights belonged to a cop car and the deer was carrying an ounce of weed. "Ed, I'm gonna tell you something," she said. "Although I got this gun in my hand, I wish you nothing but love. But if you get out of hand one more time, I would love to put a hot one in your ass. Do you understand me?" #NoMoreProblemsWithEd.

When I became a dad, teaching my kids to always have their family's back, of course, bit me in my backside. To paint the picture, because Anelise's sister, Corinne, was so much older than her (fourteen years), Anelise didn't have kids her age in my house. I wanted her to have some homies around, so when my cousins were dealing with medical issues, I invited a couple of them and their children to live with me in Westlake Village, in the valley outside LA. At first they weren't sure if they wanted to leave Texas, but they soon came to love LA and I loved having them there.

Usually the kids were well behaved, but I came home one night and saw that they had broken something in the living room. I'm no electrician or detective, but when the TV won't turn on... I know something's wrong. I went upstairs and pounded on all their doors, making them get their asses down to the living room. They all had guilty faces and tried to tell me they had homework they needed to do. *Uh-huh, homework, yeah.* So I had them all gathered, but before I could even make any accusations... they all started telling on each other! "This one did this!" "This one threw that!" Buncha SNITCHES!

That didn't sit well with me. I wanted them to learn that even if you're five years old, you have to

protect your friendships and protect your family—
to me, your friends are also your family. I told them
that no matter what, there would be no snitching
in our house. Okay, maybe that sounds like I was
operating the Westlake chapter of the Crips, but I
wanted them to develop a sense of solidarity, fellowship. Families stick together!

Of course, that policy came back to bite me in
the ass. When I was out of town, the kids found a
moment where all the adults were out the house and
thought it would be cool to take the big stand that
holds up a beanbag chair and use it like a sleigh.
But were they going to ride down one of the hills
outside? Of course not, that might cause me less
problems. Instead, they used the stand to slide down
the big curving staircase that leads from the second-
floor landing to the first floor. Yes, they treated my
fancy, expensive winding staircase like the toboggan
run in the Winter Olympics.

When I walked into the house after my trip, I saw
crazy streaks on the stairs and the wall.

"What the fuck is on my stairs?"

After they had slid down the stairs on the stand
and realized they left behind streaks, they tried to fix
it with bleach—and fucked it up even more. Not to
mention how badly they could've gotten hurt! But
also my fancy, expensive winding staircase!

I was pissed. I went to find my daughter. I

demanded that she tell me who was responsible, but she refused to squeal. In fact, she cited my very own no-snitching policy! Maybe she thought it was some kind of daddy trick to see if she would fold. Oh great, *now* you wanna listen to the lessons I teach you?!

"Anelise, what happened?" I asked.

"Can Mom be around?" she asked. She was squirming, stalling for time.

What the fuck does Mom gotta do with it? I see your tricks, you just want witnesses around for when I get to the bottom of this.

"Yeah, she can be around. But I need to know what happened to the stairs."

"Dad, we're not supposed to snitch," she said. "Besides, I didn't participate in it, and my mom knows I didn't. I said 'You guys are gonna get in trouble when my dad gets here, you know it.'"

"Well, Anelise, who all was involved?"

I tried to impress upon her that these were special circumstances. I needed a Deep Throat to give up the goods and tell me who fucked up my stairs.

She said, "It wasn't me. It wasn't PJ and it wasn't Naya." PJ and Naya are my nephew and niece who lived in the house. I don't know why she was doing this big dramatic countdown starting from who it wasn't. Maybe she felt it was less like snitching if she just told me who didn't do it and I could figure it out by process of elimination. And eventually it was clear who was the culprit. I was pissed. I didn't put a whole lot of restrictions on them. They could have respected the crib and rode the stand down the hill in the backyard, maybe just fucking up a little grass in the process.

I called all of them into the room. They lined up. I saw all the same guilty faces as in the TV incident. I didn't want to rat out Anelise for ratting them out, so I told them I was waiting for somebody to confess. And we waited. And waited. Aaaaand waited. Finally, since I can outwait any kid, they came clean. And I still scolded them about what they did, made them feel bad, but deep down, I was kinda proud they learned a lesson about having their family's back.

I didn't love that it was at the expense of that beautiful staircase though!

THE GIFT THAT KEEPS ON GIVING

Estelle and Mark Talley hailed from this tiny town of 12,000, with one movie theater and seven stoplights. (If you remember, I said there were six before. They added a seventh, it was a big deal.) But somehow they knew how to cultivate big city dreams. Probably because of *Jet* magazine and *Ebony* magazine. *Ebony* and *Jet* was how all Black folks got the 411 on what was happening in the world. Those magazines were how we learned about entertainers making it in showbiz. Black entertainers were doing their thing (the Temptations, the Jackson 5, Sidney Poitier, Richard Pryor, etc.), and they always believed that I had the same sauce to become a star. While they often disciplined me (aka whupped my ass), they made sure to never limit my imagination. Black discipline is a delicate mathematical equation—you gotta whup just enough to scare but not enough to crush the creative spirit. Two plus two is four, and a two-by-four might be too hard to smack a kid around with.

I was a smart kid, if I do say so myself. My grandmother had a library filled with books. I blasted through Dr. Seuss (way before we knew about his racist ass) and moved on to the classics. I drank up the knowledge in those books so fast—*To Kill a Mockingbird*, *The Great Gatsby*, *Moby-Dick*, my grandmother even made me read the dictionary once (I never got past the Cs but you never wanna see me in a game of Scrabble). By the time I got to second and third grade, I was so far ahead of the class that I think I was bored. Back in the '70s we didn't yet know what ADD was, but when I think about it now, I'm fairly certain I had a touch of it. The way it showed up was me acting somewhat rambunctious in class. But I wasn't just acting up in the regular ways; I was becoming a stand-up comedian. I had a knack for emulation. I would often imitate my teachers and they rarely found the portrayals flattering—probably because they weren't. And the imitations didn't stop at teachers.

There wasn't a day when I wasn't regurgitating jokes I heard on *The Tonight Show* to my classmates and teachers—and it was constantly getting me in trouble. We didn't have a lot of space at home, so my bedroom also served as the TV room where my grandmother watched the Johnny Carson show every night (yeah, she did watch more than just Lawrence Welk). This meant I would have to stay up and watch it with her, well past what should have been my bedtime. But by doing that, I was absorbing the science of stand-up comedy. Watching Richard Pryor, I learned that you didn't have to censor yourself, you could be bold and raw. Watching Redd Foxx, I was able to hone my storytelling abilities. Nobody told a story quite like Redd Foxx.

I would try out my act on my grandmother, who would enjoy watching me acting the fool around the house, repeating the jokes and the routines I saw on television. She was a tough critic—"Oh, you think you're so funny? Let's see how funny you are doing the dishes"—so it meant something to me to make her laugh. The typical joking around wouldn't cut it; you had to really catch her off guard to get her laughing, but then you'd earn a real hearty belly laugh.

Because she could see the gift I had, she let all of Terrell know, every chance she got, that everybody needed to help her nurture this gift. I know, I know, every parent thinks their kid is special, but she was the loudest about it. She even went to my teachers and essentially apologized in advance for my behavior because she knew I was going to be a challenge for them.

In third grade my teacher, Miss Reeves, had no idea what she was in store for. She was a young, new teacher who wasn't beaten down by the school system—or by the class clown—yet. Eventually she gave up trying to control me—instead she wisely brokered a deal.

Miss Reeves said, "Eric, you're disrupting my class and I can't have that. But at the same time, you make me laugh out loud. At the end of every class on Friday, I'll give you ten minutes to do your thing."

Thank God for Miss Reeves.

All week I would just wait and wait for Friday. Counting down the days, hours, minutes. I would be thinking all week about what I was going to say at the next performance (even if I'd often end up winging it anyway). Sometimes it was tough to behave in class, but even at that age, I understood a deal is a deal, and if I wanted those ten minutes, I had to shut the fuck up when Miss Reeves was teaching.

Those ten minutes turned into twenty minutes, and eventually those twenty minutes turned into sometimes full days of me doing my stand-up—saying jokes I had heard on *The Tonight Show*, doing a lot of impersonations of President Jimmy Carter. And eventually doing actual jokes, like Jimmy Carter singing "You Light Up My Life."

So many nights, me and my brother Billy would sit
  by the window
Waiting for someone to bring us peanuts and
  beer...

All the kids laughed. They thought I was brilliant and original, even though sometimes I would just be copying things I'd picked up from some of the greatest comedians the world had ever seen: Franklyn Ajaye, David Brenner, Johnny Carson, young David Letterman, Steve Martin, Rich Little, Richard Pryor, Flip Wilson, Sammy Davis Jr.... The list goes on and on. I wanted to one day be like those people I saw on that little box; I would let my ambitions be known at school, telling everyone I was going to be a star. Pretty soon word got around, and teachers from the elementary school, middle school and high school would crowd into my fifth grade class to watch me do my routines.

"You have to go see Estelle Talley's son," the teachers would tell each other. "It's like watching *The Tonight Show* in real life."

Then, as you know, there was the music. Granny told me she had always liked music. There was always B.B. King or Aretha Franklin playing. She couldn't play herself, but when I was in elementary school she said she wanted me to learn classical piano. First of all, I didn't even wanna play music—I wanted to play outside with my friends. But if I did have to play music…why classical piano?! You think a Black kid in the South would get excited about *classical piano*? I wanted to play Little Richard, Billy Preston, Stevie Wonder, Ray Charles. (I did happen to end up playing Ray Charles but that was a bit more down the road.)

"It could take you on the other side of the tracks," she said.

"You want me to go play for white people?"

"No, boy. The metaphoric tracks." She went on to explain that music connects us all and I'd be able to travel the world. I was a little young to comprehend how much music brought people together, but right away I liked the sound of connecting with people. And I definitely liked the sound of traveling the world. Aruba, Jamaica, I couldn't wait to get there. Bermuda, Bahama, come on, pretty—well, you get it. I wanted to see the world.

Now, she had her reasons for wanting me to play; I had mine. And what often motivates young boys? Yup. *Women.* It started with Uncle Talley, my mother's brother, who Granny had also adopted—so technically he was my uncle/brother. One day I saw Talley, who was seven years older than me, come in the house with this girl named Debbie. She was a beautiful, full-figured, light-skinned girl. She had a cool asymmetrical hairstyle going on and was rocking a pair of Daisy Dukes that showed just enough to get your imagination going. He brought her into the room where the piano was, which we called the Blue Room. He didn't see me hiding behind the couch; he was just focused on impressing Debbie. She said, "Talley, play that music for me."

Talley started playing the piano. Then they lit up a funny-looking cigarette. I didn't know what it was—all I know is I went outside and played for about five hours after I sat there inhaling it. Talley started playing and Debbie started swooning. Then he spotted me.

"Get the fuck out of here, Eric! I need some time alone with Debbie."

I wasn't sure what he meant, but it sounded like some furniture was being rearranged in the room when I left. From that moment, seeing how Debbie reacted to the piano, I told myself I had to get serious about it—no more half-assing the piano lessons. As that Malcolm Gladwell book *Outliers* says, you gotta put ten thousand hours into something to become great at it, and I was ready to put in eleven thousand because it's no secret I love women—big ones, small ones, Black ones, white ones, even blue ones (that tall, freaky alien from *Avatar* could GET IT). And, of course, the player's curse is having two daughters. Every time my daughters would meet a guy who had any musical talent, I'd tell them, "Don't buy into it! He only learned that to impress you!"

My grandmother found a woman from Dallas named LaNita Hodge to teach me. She was a cigarette-smoking drill sergeant of a piano teacher. She was like Sergeant Carter, Lou Gossett Jr. and the dude from *Full Metal Jacket* all wrapped in one. She was mean and had a face to match. She taught me the discipline of piano, scales and, as my grandma intended, had me play classical music.

"Don't let me see you deviate from playing that," she told me sternly. She told me with her words and also told me with a switch that she would hit my hands with. And I'm talking about a real thin switch, the kind you had to peel the skin off. Went *whap!* She was the female Joe Jackson. I never understood that logic. You want me to play piano with broken fingers?!

My grandmother had convinced Miss Hodge to drive to Terrell by telling her she would enlist a bunch of kids in the town to come to our house for lessons. Soon my house was the meeting point of young aspiring artists. I got close with a lot of them and, ever since, it's been important to me to always be surrounded by artists. No disrespect to my friends from the football team but, goddamn, you get a bunch of creatives together and shit happens. It's hard to explain that synergy that forms with artists being in a room together. It always stuck with me, even in the future when I got a house in California and I would invite all sorts of talented folks (Brian McKnight, Tank, you name it) to roll through and play music.

But back to Terrell: Even though my grandmother wanted me to focus on classical piano, she ironically set up a situation where I was getting drawn to way more than classical music. Due to spending time with these other artists, I started to grow as I was exposed to the different types of music they were playing. I was blown away—jazz, R&B, stride...I began to color outside the lines, to take the principles of all those musical genres and see what I could create on my own.

I was also forced to play piano at church, but I would always bomb. And you don't wanna bomb in church, because that means you're bombing in front of God and he'll remember that shit when you're up at the Pearly Gates. There was this guy Paul Jackson (he was a football star, a musician...motherfucker could do anything), and he broke down for me what wasn't working. In the Black church, you can't just play by the music, you gotta *take 'em to church*—that is, add enough soul-stirring rhythms that they get filled with the spirit and get the hell up from their seats and move, calling out their praise for the Lord! But I didn't know how to do that. There I was, trying to play "What a Friend We Have in Jesus" by the sheet music, putting their asses to sleep. Paul was witnessing me go down in flames in front of the pastor and the congregation. At one point the pastor even prayed for me, that I would learn how to play better in church—if not, everybody was going to hell because of how terrible I was playing. Paul walked up to me and graciously said, "You need some chords."

"What?"

"When you playin', you need chords."

He showed me what chording was and taught me how to play church music. I graduated from that to playing music I heard on the radio, like songs by Lionel Richie. When I was in eighth grade, I played "Hello" in front of my classmates. I grew a California curl and everything. The way Debbie swooned with Talley was the way all the girls were swooning in class. I'm sorry, Grandma, but I didn't think the girls were gonna be feeling Mozart like that.

So music and stand-up became an elemental part of who I am; I became a performer. When my own children started showing an interest in music and performing, my smile was several miles wide. However, I also felt a bit of trepidation. The entertainment industry obviously has been pretty good to me, but I know firsthand that the business is not easy. Just as soon as it wraps its arms around you, it can push you away.

I saw that Corinne might be leaning toward going into the entertainment business long before she did. The way she was always performing, putting on dance shows, I just saw it (and eventually she would admit to me I was right). Obviously I would support her no matter what she wanted to do— "You sure you wanna be a bank robber, baby? Okay, you do you, girl, don't leave any witnesses"— but it's scary thinking about your daughter trying to make it in show business. That said, as she got older, it just became clear that, like me, that's what she was meant for. Not only is she a beautiful girl, but she appeared to have some real talent.

I directed her in a sizzle reel when she was a teenager. It was something we did for an idea I had called Amber Alert, about a task force who hunts for missing children. We shot it at my house and she played the dispatcher and also a field agent. There was no script; I just explained what we were trying to do. Right away I saw that she had the eyes. When actors can act with their eyes, they engage and somehow immediately make you feel like they have become that person. I saw that and I said to myself, *Oh wow. She has it.*

And I know, I know, you're reading this thinking,

"Of course this guy thinks his daughter is amazing, she's his daughter!" Well, you're goddamn right. She's my daughter and this is my book and Corinne is fucking talented.

"Dad, I felt it," she told me. So I did what any dad has to do—supported my daughter. My grandma saw something in me and I saw something in her. And I encouraged her to get into acting.

The biggest acting advice I gave her (during that sizzle and in the future) was to not overthink things. To be in the moment. She would always tell me that's easy for me to say. I guess it's one of those things where you have to overthink and overprepare for a long time until finally you're able to stop thinking about acting and let it flow out naturally, be playful in the moment. Sometimes I don't fully read the script before I get to set so I can truly be in the moment. I don't know if the director always loves that, but don't worry about me, I'll crush it.

But back to Corinne. She acted here and there but it hadn't become her primary focus yet. She wanted to go to college. We actually got into a bit of a tiff because I thought she should just go right into an acting career. In retrospect, not a proud dad moment. In my defense, I think I had memories of my grandmother in the back of my mind—when you see talent, you nurture it, you try to keep that light burning.

"You don't need college, you got Hollywood," said no parent ever—except one named Jamie Foxx.

When I said that, she gave me the same look she had at the airport when I didn't have an ID to pick her up—except now she was old enough to be thinking *This muthafucka!* Her mother, Connie, was a good counterbalance to me and (shockingly) supported our daughter getting a college education.

I'm so glad Corinne didn't follow my lead. She ended up going to USC, which made me so proud. When I brought her to campus to move in, we took a minute to stand in front of the dorms and frat houses and check out the scene. Just then, a kid stumbled past us and collapsed on the ground. Passed the fuck out. He had probably been at a frat party all night.

Corinne gasped. "Oh my God, Dad! What is that?!"

I chuckled. "Hey, it's college, baby."

Corinne took college very seriously. Considering all the USC graduates killing it in Hollywood— from Ron Howard to Will Ferrell, John Singleton to Paula Patton—I realized she had made a great decision by starting off there.

After college, Corinne got a job in New York working nine to five at an ad agency, and then I got The Call. I got to hear those sweet words, "Dad... you were right." Corinne told me she didn't want to work behind a desk the rest of her life. She was ready to get serious about acting. And I had to tell her how serious she had to get. "Actors would *die* to get the job," I told her. If she wanted to pursue this, she needed to dedicate herself fully to it. Acting classes, managers, the works.

After she left advertising and decided to pursue an acting career, she came to me and said she wanted to do it on her own—starting with using a different last name.

"Huh? What do you mean?"

"Dad, you don't get it!" she said. "I'm independent!"

I shook my head. "That's great, Corinne. But why did you go to USC? So that whenever you go to get a job, you can always say, 'I went to USC.'"

I looked at her closely. "Well, Corinne, in Hollywood I'm your USC. When you're going into *this* world, having me as a father's an asset."

Before I ever thought about being a dad, I had been working hard to make a name for myself. After Corinne came along, I wanted to put things in place so that she would be surrounded by people in the industry who would be more than happy to help her if she ever decided to follow my path. Eventually she let go of the idea of changing her name, but she didn't let go of her insistence on independence. She wouldn't tell me when she went on auditions, and she never asked me to make any phone calls on her behalf. And then if she didn't get that part, I would feel more rejected than she did. *Like what the hell? You would think I would be used to rejection after thirty years in this business.*

It goes without saying, you want your kids to succeed. So when your kid is in a field like entertainment, it's a total roller coaster. When she booked a part, I was that dad in the stands when their kid hits a home run in Little League—I'm screaming loud as hell, embarrassing her. And when things didn't go well, I just had to be there for her. I wanted to change the rain for her, to remove the clouds from her skies so it's sunshine all day. But you can't dictate the weather for your kids. Sometimes it's gonna rain on them—and that's okay. Just bring an umbrella. And don't fly a kite if there's lightning.

And guess what? Corinne started blowing the fuck up. At the end of 2019, it all came to a head for me when she landed a starring role in the live version of *Good Times*. Her living, breathing legacy was right there on the screen. I was thrilled and terrified at the same time. I had just done a live show earlier in 2019, playing George Jefferson on *The Jeffersons*— and famously flubbing a line. Jimmy Kimmel, who had brilliantly reprised these classic comedies, called me to let me know Corinne had gotten the role of Thelma—who just happened to be the object of every Black boy's fantasies in the 1970s. I was like,

"Damn, that's great, but can't you give her a role that wasn't a sex symbol—like maybe a nun that just moved into their building?!"

I knew the part could wind up being the best thing to happen to Corinne's career—or it could be the worst thing if it didn't go so well. But as the day of the production approached, Corinne seemed to have no fear. It was as if after all those years of being on sets, watching the entertainment sausage being made, witnessing the business end of the craft, somehow a fearlessness about the big moment had seeped in. I was a nervous wreck on her behalf—I was pacing around like I had a Venti Starbucks with extra shots plugged into my veins. Corinne had to calm me down. You know you've done a good job parenting your kid when they start parenting you.

On the day of the show, I was grateful that I had to do an appearance on *Jimmy Kimmel Live!* That took me away from the studio where they were performing *Good Times* and *All in the Family* live before a studio audience. I wouldn't have to fight off the fear of having a nervous breakdown in front of a legion of my industry colleagues who were there to watch it all. Instead, I had my near nervous breakdown in the car on the way to the studio after leaving Kimmel's set across town. As the limo driver crept through traffic, seemingly going extra slow, my friends were calling and texting me with updates

ACT LIKE YOU GOT SOME SENSE 93

on her performance. Their reviews were overwhelmingly positive. My boy Johnny Mack called and said, "Foxx, your daughter's a star." He didn't call me when *Miami Vice* came out, so I knew this was legit.

My friend and assistant Dave was watching the show on his phone from the front seat. Every time he turned around with the phone in his hand to show me, I told him I didn't want to see it. I just couldn't stand it. And I was hungry to hear from Dave and anybody else to tell me how my baby girl was doing. It truly was one of the most nerve-racking nights of my life. I was legitimately petrified. What if she messed up? After all, I had messed up a few months earlier. I had given her a ton of advice about the wisdom of being exceptionally prepared while still trying to stay in the moment—but what if she hadn't listened to me? Oh God, a failure here could sink her career just as it was getting off the ground.

Of course, Corinne once again killed it. It felt like a passing of the baton—a baton that Estelle Talley had somehow created out of thin air in Terrell and pressed into my hand. There were of course some minor differences between my and Corinne's upbringings. I grew up dirt poor in public school, Corinne went to nice private schools. She grew up in a liberal, progressive paradise. I was like a track runner with no shoes, she had the best track shoes that money could buy. But she still had to show up to the track, she still had to train hard and a baton is a baton.

Even though Granny was no longer with us, much of the joy I felt was on her behalf. She's probably still up there smiling, knowing her hard work paid off. And that I took enough ass beatings for both me and her great-granddaughter.

LESS MONEY,
MO' PROBLEMS!

My grandmother had the ability to see the future. She knew the piano wouldn't just be a hobby for me; she could tell I would be taking the piano to the bank (not literally, because pianos are very difficult to transport). I first started making some dollars with my piano playing when the church started paying me a nice salary of seventy-five dollars a week. That's three hundred dollars a month! That might not sound like a lot to you now—that's maybe enough for a few decent shirts and a niceish pair of pants. But to a teenager in 1980?! Shit, that's a whole new fly outfit with enough pocket change to take your girl out, take your girl's best friend out *and* take your girl out again to apologize for taking her best friend out. I spent a lot of time in that church playing piano, and no matter how many questions I had about God or the afterlife, I knew in this life it was money in my pocket. #PraiseTheLord.

When I got that job, you couldn't beat me to church on Sunday to play for the service. You couldn't beat me on Wednesday for junior choir practice. You couldn't beat me on Thursday for regular choir practice. I played the piano for Jesus and He paid me well. But guess what? My grandmother was like the government—she was taxing my ass. She was taxing at the rate of 100 percent. Every dollar I got, she would take it from me.

"Didn't you get paid this week?" she'd ask.

"Yeah."

"Well, hand it over."

I don't know why the hell I allowed this to happen. I guess because I didn't have a choice. I kept thinking maybe this was the week she'd give me a cut of my own money, but nope. She'd take my dough and make another deposit in her special bank—Titty Bank Federal. She put it right in her chest. And she never gave me any of it. Every single cent, from age thirteen all the way to age eighteen when I went away to college. I couldn't ever get her to budge off a nickel. Do the math—we're talking thousands of dollars. Eventually she did give it to me (keep reading) but at the time, I was pissed!

At a certain point it would wear on me. I would want to go do things with kids, go to the teenage club in Garland, Texas, called Fast Times. Dancing, loud mouthin'—it was *the Spot*! But if I did go there I would have to borrow money, as if I still didn't have a job. One day I confronted her.

"Granny, why do you always take the money I make and give me none of it?"

"Do you pay rent?" she asked me.

"No."

"Do you pay electricity bills?"

"No."

"Then when you get your own house, your own bills, you can have your own money. Until then, it's going into Titty Bank Federal."

Okay, she didn't actually say that last sentence— but that's what I heard.

As my high school years went by, I started to build up a bit of animosity toward my grandmother. It was like she had me working in a piano sweatshop. I would have to go find little odd jobs to scrape together a few dollars. I would keep those jobs hidden so my grandma couldn't tax my income. I do *not* recommend trying this with the federal government.

But my grandmother was viewing piano as way more than just a way to make money. And it ended up becoming my artistic ticket to go to college. My grandmother had helped raise a kid who was about four years older than me and attending United States International University in San Diego. She reached out to him on my behalf. She told him, "Maybe my baby would like to go there. I'd like to see him get out of this town."

He set me up with an audition and I soon found out I had won a classical piano scholarship. *Holy shit!* Every emotion was running through my head at once. Obviously I was excited to move to a new place, a big city with who knows what there. But it's a little scary leaving your small, comfortable, safe hometown. I didn't even know anyone in San Diego. And then I realized I'd probably already met every girl in Terrell and how many new girls there would be in San Diego, and I got excited again.

It was scary at first but I started to meet people and have a good time. I got a job at International playing piano for dance class and used my earnings to buy a Triumph TR7. Oh baby, I couldn't tell you how bad I wanted that Triumph! You couldn't tell me nuthin'—until the Triumph broke down. I didn't have the money to get it repaired, so I had to leave it in the parking lot at the college. I finally got enough money together to get the Triumph fixed, and I was flying high again! Until the cops pulled me over...

"What's up, officer?" I mentally did a check of the

car. I was 90 percent positive there wasn't any weed in the vehicle. Was I speeding? Honestly, probably. But that wasn't it.

"Um, you have six hundred dollars' worth of outstanding parking tickets," he said.

"But that's impossible!" I said. "My car's been parked in the university lot."

The officer informed me that the car had been accumulating tickets while sitting in the lot; the school had turned those tickets over to the city. That's pretty fucked up if you ask me. To attend college, you have to either pay a bunch of money, go into serious debt or grow up dirt poor and work your way up with a scholarship. Either way, don't make these students pay for *parking* on top of it all. You got a big-ass lot and collect so much tuition, give us free parking! Even the fucked-up, dirty game of Monopoly gives out free parking!

"We gotta take the car," the officer said.

"What?!"

They actually drove my car away, leaving me standing by the side of the damn road. It was cold-blooded. I had to walk a couple miles back to school, wondering the whole time what I was going to do. It had taken every dime I possessed to get the car fixed. I didn't have a cent. I calculated in my head that it would take a year of ballet-class piano playing to get my car back. I was messed up. I broke down and called my grandmother, already sobbing when she answered the phone.

"They took the car, Granny!" I said, trying to get out the words between racking sobs. "Six hundred dollars in parking tickets! The police said—"

"Boy, who took the car?"

"The Triumph!" Sob sob. "They need money!" Sob sob. "I ain't got it!"

"Boy, if you don't shut up!"

"Granny, they got my car! I had it in the parking lot."

"Well, what you saying?"

"Granny, I need six hundred something dollars."

"Well, I'm gonna tell you something," she said. "I know you think I was a hard-ass all these years, taking your money and everything. But I took that money and put it into an account. And right now you have $7,500 in there. I put it away for you because I knew you was gonna spend it going to the clubs and all that kinda stuff. But here's the thing: You grown now, and I'm going to turn it over to you."

I couldn't believe what I was hearing. I'm crying as I type this now, thinking about it. She really did care about me! As a matter of fact, I still have money in that account, American National Bank in Terrell, as a reminder and a tribute of sorts to my grandmother.

As much as I want to provide my girls with *everything*, I remember to try to instill the same principles in them. No, I didn't want my daughters growing up poor, but I also didn't need them growing up spoiled! I am always on hyperalert for any signs that my daughters (or even any of their cousins) are taking their privilege for granted. I am quick with all of them to snatch stuff away if I get any inkling of bullshit.

During Christmas a couple years ago, Anelise and her cousins were opening gifts and my head exploded when I heard one of them say, out loud, "I'm tired of opening presents." I can't remember which child it was, but they all shared the same sentiment. They had so many gifts to open that the effort to pull away the wrapping paper was tiring them out. *Are you kidding me?* Y'all tired of…OPENING PRESENTS?! I'm so sorry, children. I greatly apologize for busting my ass, making money, to buy you all this bullshit. I went in.

"Really? Y'all tired, huh? Well, just wait and see what next Christmas looks like!"

I started to blame myself for their reaction. Sure, if you grow up where the normal is having everything, it's difficult to learn to appreciate anything. So when Christmas approached the next year, I told them things would be different. At first, I was so mad that I considered getting them jack shit. Or a lump of coal each and blame it on Santa. But once I cooled off, I had a better idea. I limited each of them to only one or two gifts that were actually meaningful. There was not going to be a pile of expensive presents scattered all over the room, looking like a wrapping paper factory had exploded. And it worked out great. The kids learned the meaning of Christmas isn't the gifts but the meaning and people behind the gifts. And I needed that reminder myself. I realized just because I could afford to buy them a million presents doesn't mean I shouldn't stop and reflect and make sure I was putting thought into what I was getting them. Yeah, I know, I'm coming to the same realization that happens at the end of any Christmas movie. But hey, they're clichés for a reason—because it's easy to get caught up in life and forget.

And they finally learned to appreciate getting an expensive gift. Or so I thought. One day my daughter and her cousins came to me, desperate to get fancy cameras. They wanted to produce some kind of video blog, which I guess you call a vlog. Remembering my grandmother always nurturing my creative side, I agreed that it was a worthwhile purchase, so I went out and bought very nice Sonys, which each cost well over $500. Goddamn, did I ever own anything growing up that cost $500?! Even $100 was a stretch.

Within a week, the cameras had been set aside. I would walk by every day and see them sitting in the same spot, gathering dust. Where the hell were all these vlogs I was promised? But the kids had moved on to some other preoccupation, the Sonys and the vlog long forgotten. *Oh, we got the cameras, we dug that for thirty minutes, time for the next thing.* That's very much consistent with the world they live in, precisely how things work on social media. Always time to move on to the next. So I was trying to teach them about the value of expensive gifts and now I have to teach them about discipline and seeing things through?! Damn, you really gotta teach kids everything. I know these kids aren't spoiled, but everyone needs a reminder now and then.

I finally got my chance to make a statement when they came back to me, talking about how they needed microphones to go with the Sony cameras. "You're not getting that," I said. "I told you I wanted to see you using those cameras, but now I never see the cameras. You have to stick to things." They bitched and moaned, but once I saw some vlogs rolling in, I got them some mics.

Now, I stand by this previous story as a *parent*, but if there are any aspiring *filmmakers* reading this book, here's a quick tip. Audio is ten thousand times more important than video. So when you're starting out and wanna make your own shit, worry about getting a decent microphone before spending too much on a camera. Do a little experiment and click through YouTube right now. I bet you'll be willing to keep watching a video that doesn't look the best. But something that *sounds* like shit? You're turning that the fuck off. Okay, back to parenting...

I regularly insert some type of bigger lesson about discipline when I'm with Anelise. If you want to go to Disneyland, you have to take five hundred jump shots first. Once in a while I find it necessary to make adjustments to the lens the kids are looking through. We checked into a hotel and they complained some of the kids had to share a bed. I sat them down and explained that most people don't ever get a chance to lay their head in such spaces. It's about being together and that's what matters.

Sometimes I feel like the gestapo on this issue because it's so important to me. It's one thing not to be able to give your kids something because you can't afford it; it's another if you *can* afford it but don't get it for them to prove a point. You gotta be a little coldhearted about it. If you have a pet, you know this game—your puppy looking up at you with the cutest marble eyes begging for a snack. *No, motherfucker, I already fed you! You want me to keep feeding you until you're a big-ass chonker and can't even walk?!*

I know how much it could affect the rest of their

lives if I let them emerge from childhood with that sense of entitlement permanently embedded in their psyches. All I have to do is look around me in Hollywood to see what that would look like. Rich kids who were born on third base and act like they hit a triple. Also, the fear of slipping is constantly with me. Thank God I'm still able to work in the industry, but what happens if people no longer want to buy tickets to see me in movies or don't buy a book I wrote (thank you again for making this book purchase)? I better make sure when my kids are grown, they value the hard work instead of just getting used to having a lot of money.

I think I did a pretty good job with Corinne in that sense. She was always disgusted with ostentatious displays of wealth. But also, on the flip side, I grew up poor, remember? So sometimes I get carried away with spending money. Haven't I literally earned it? May I treat myself a little?! There was one evening where the roles were reversed...with a Rolls-Royce.

There I was one evening after a football game at Corinne's high school, picking her up after she put in a full Friday night as head of the cheerleading squad. I had just gotten my hands on a sleek new black Rolls-Royce convertible. Oh, it was purty. A scene like this was always a dream of mine, picking up my baby girl at the fancy school populated with all the rich white folks. What teenager wouldn't love that, right? Well, you know the answer. *Corinne.* My very reserved, very sensible teenage daughter, Corinne.

I slid the shiny black car into the pickup line and moved along with the other cars. Her high school is a co-ed private school that had established a reputation as a school of choice for the Hollywood elite. Basically it's a fancy-pants school. Celeb and rich kids all through those halls. In other words, I figured these kids were used to a certain amount of luxury; I wouldn't look ridiculous pulling up in my new Rolls-Royce.

But when I got to the front of the pickup line and saw the look of horror on my daughter's face, I started to realize I had fucked up.

"Dad!" Corinne screeched. "What are you doing?!"

Immediately, I panicked. Maybe she just needed to see how cool it was.

"Look, Corinne, the top goes down!" I said. Wrong!

Corinne looked around at her friends, who seemed to be enjoying the whole spectacle. My daughter wasn't having it.

"You're embarrassing me. I'm not getting in that!" she said. It wasn't helping that I was blasting loud hip-hop music.

I started to get flustered. Was there anything I could do to save face?

"C'mon, Corinne, get in," I said, gently, trying the softer approach, turning the music down a little. But she was already on her phone.

"Mom, can you come get me?" she said. "Dad's trying to pick me up in a ship."

I was mortified. The girl actually refused to get in the car with me. I couldn't believe it. How could I have made such a massive miscalculation? Corinne fled the scene, leaving me there looking like a goofball in the gaudy car. But when I realized why she was embarrassed, I knew I had done an alright job raising her.

But while Corinne wasn't about the flash and the glitz at all, from day one it was clear that Anelise preferred it. Let me explain this. She had no idea what was glitz and what was regular. All she saw was what's sitting in the driveway—and what's the shiniest. When she was still in Pull-Ups, she was already displaying her love of flair, personified most perfectly by Rihanna, her favorite artist at the time. While she was adjusting her training pants, she'd be throwing Rihanna's diamond sign in the air.

On one particular day I had an important meeting scheduled, but I was watching Anelise so I had to take her with me. When we walked out to the driveway where all the cars were lined up, I asked her which one she wanted to take. I wanted to take the Rolls, but the incident at Corinne's high school was still fresh in my mind. I figured it was a good move to let my baby girl choose.

She extended her finger almost like a slow-motion scene. In my head I heard a drumroll.

"That one right there!" she said.

Oh, that's my baby! I thought.

We jumped in the Rolls, dropped the top back, put her in the baby seat, popped Rihanna on the stereo and hit the 101. If you know anything about Cali, you know the 101 is prime time when it comes to announcing your status to people. We flew by the palm trees in Thousand Oaks and I cracked up when I looked back at Anelise. She had on her hat, her shades, and she was clutching her favorite doll. The perfect little Hollywood toddler. As we drove down Sunset Boulevard, it almost felt like Anelise could sense how iconic the street was. In Beverly Hills her hands went up in the air as she sang along to RiRi.

As we pulled up into the driveway of our destination, I felt the need to have a brief talk with my little one. The meeting was taking place at Soho House. It's an exclusive private club in LA for industry players. I wasn't a member of the club, but I knew ostentation was not welcomed. After all, I'm just a country boy wanting to show off his toys, but these people were all about driving a Prius and pretending their net worth wasn't a number with two commas in it—rich people trying to act like they're normal.

"Look, Anelise," I said. "We're pulling up to the Soho House and we're riding in a Rolls-Royce. It's kind of big and sort of gaudy, you know. It may not be a good look to ride in there like this, because most of these people drive Priuses."

A shadow crossed her face. She didn't like where this was going, like someone had canceled her Instagram account.

"Why?" she asked.

"It's just not a good look," I repeated.

As we drove into the parking lot of Soho House, the Hollywood elite were already visible. I told her to play it cool, and I started to put the top on the convertible—I guess I was thinking maybe they wouldn't be able to see me then. But my theory wasn't put to the test because I hadn't exactly clarified what "playing it cool" meant to Anelise. Before I could get the top all the way on, she got up out of her seat and screamed . . . "Jamie Foxx in the house!"

Anelise had no interest in being subdued. She wanted everyone to know who had just arrived. I saw a bunch of white people look out at us. I'm sure there was a bunch of whispered talk.

"Look at Jamie Foxx, trying to do too much." She didn't actually know it was a Rolls-Royce. She was too young to know what Sunset Boulevard or Soho House was. She was just chillin' with Dad.

So what's the lesson about money? Having it

is great. Not having it is tough. But having it and still teaching your kids the value of it is also tough. And while you're teaching your kids all this, you still wanna have fun with it and create great memories with your kids because...you only live once. So it's a delicate balance, but of course I'd rather have some money in my pocket than not. It's not *all* about the Benjamins but it's nice when Benjamin is rolling in your entourage.

IT TAKES A VILLAGE

It's true that it takes a village to raise a child, but I think it goes beyond the perimeters of just the one village. Growing up, the child wanders through different villages, and people who happen to live there and don't even know the child end up being a major influence on them.

Hollywood was another (slightly larger) village I ended up at, and I would be remiss if I wrote this parenting book and didn't mention some people who were my entertainment parents, so to speak.

When I first came to Hollywood, I was like everybody else who comes here: I wanted to be a star. I was still a college student in San Diego, and one of my uncles reached out to me on campus one day with a phone call that started me on my path.

"Boy, you trying to do this singing thing, you need to be heard by the right people," he said. "You know who Marvin Gaye is?"

"Yeah, of course," I said. "Who doesn't?"

"Well, I know Marvin Gaye's manager."

At the time, I thought my uncle was just putting me on, trying to be a big shot. But I desperately needed any connection I could get to try to break into Hollywood, so I bought into it. Turns out he was telling the truth. He really did know Harvey Fuqua—who was a good singer but an even more impressive producer. This dude was responsible for Etta James, Tammi Terrell, New Birth, Sylvester and, if that wasn't enough, *Marvin Gaye!* He had just produced Marvin's last album when Marvin was killed by his father in 1984. And even though a few years had passed, Harvey was still in mourning. Hell, I was still in mourning and I never even knew Marvin.

Superexcited to meet him, I drove all the way up to Dorothy Street in Brentwood, blasting Marvin Gaye. When I got up to the apartment, still a little skeptical, I looked at the mailbox. It read FUQUA/GAYE/FREEMAN. Could this really be true? It was my first time interacting with any sort of celebrity and I was already starstruck looking at a fucking mailbox!

I knocked on the door and a tall, distinguished, older Black man answered.

He immediately asked me, "You the young fella that sings?"

"Yes, sir," I said. A little jarring, but I've never cared about small talk and respected someone diving right into it.

"You see that over there to the left?"

I turned my head in the direction he was pointing.

"That's Marvin Gaye's reel-to-reels and keyboards. You know anything about it?"

I didn't know the technical side but I knew how to play piano and I definitely knew how much magic was made with these keys! This was the piano Marvin wrote "What's Going On" on! I hid how nervous I was and how shaky my fingers were and just started playing, and I nervously began singing. I could not believe that I was let within ten miles of Marvin Gaye's keyboard, let alone was allowed to touch it. I kept peeking over at Harvey, waiting for him to tell me that I wasn't shit. Yet, every time I'd look, he was nodding along. He even closed his eyes, and he later told me he imagined his friend Marvin was back in the room with him.

That was the beginning of a strange relationship. I would drive from San Diego to Harvey's house every weekend and sometimes stay there, acting occasionally as his assistant—taking calls, running errands and so on. But mostly I was there to play and sing Marvin Gaye songs for him or for guests he was entertaining. He clearly was still in pain over losing Marvin. It felt a little weird, like when I would play "Let's Get It On" just for him, but I went along because I hoped it would lead to something. I knew I had to let him know that I wanted to create my own art as well, that this wasn't it for me. I was hungry and ready to be part of any scene.

And the hottest scene at the time was stand-up comedy—Eddie Murphy, Richard Pryor, Jerry Seinfeld, George Carlin, these guys were bigger rock stars than actual rock stars. Music is in my heart, but stand-up is in my blood. One weekend when I told Harvey I couldn't play Marvin Gaye songs all night because I had to go to a club to do stand-up, he was taken aback.

"You do stand-up?"

"Yeah."

"Oh, so you funny, huh?" he asked.

"I'm funny as a motherfucker," I answered, a little annoyed. You haven't just heard me sing, Harvey. I've cracked you up.

"Okay. Well, we'll see if you're funny." He put on a tough exterior, but he genuinely wanted to see if I had other talents and help me out if he could.

Harvey hooked up an appearance for me at the Comedy Act Theater, which was located in the

Regency West building near Crenshaw. In other words, it was in the hood. It wasn't my first time onstage but this was the biggest venue I had ever performed at. I knew that if I could kill it at the Comedy Act Theater, where the audiences were savage (it was the West Coast version of the Apollo), I could make it anywhere.

The Comedy Act Theater had been booming solely because of one man, Robin Harris, who was the king in that space. On the night I was to go up, Harvey called a few Hollywood industry types to come watch, including Robi Reed, the casting director who was casting all of Spike Lee's movies. When I got there, I sat at a table by myself, with my Jheri curl drying up because I didn't have enough money to fix it. There were a couple of beautiful Black girls sitting at the table next to me. I tried to strike up a conversation with them because I'm naturally a gregarious motherfucker.

"Hey, how y'all doing?" I said. "Y'all come here all the time?"

They shunned me. I understood. It's LA and I ain't got no résumé.

The owner of the club, Michael Williams, came to get me. "Come on, you gonna be the first one on!" he said. First?! Shit, that was a lot of pressure going up first. Even worse than just being first, Robin Harris was hosting, so in a sense I'd be following a legend.

Michael sat next to me in the back of the club while Robin did his thing onstage. "You see what he doin'?" he said.

"Who doin'?" I asked cluelessly.

"Robin Harris. You see what he doin'?"

"Yeah, he telling jokes," I said.

"No. He ain't," Michael said. "He kickin' they motherfuckin' ass. That's what you got to do for niggas. You can't just be funny. You gotta whup they goddamn ass!" It reminded me of when Paul Jackson told me I couldn't just play piano at church, I had to take 'em to church! I knew exactly what he meant—and how to do it.

But he wasn't thinking about my set, his mind was already on something else (aka money) as he looked around the club. "It's a two-drink minimum and I don't let nobody slide."

As he was talking, a server walked by with a shrimp basket. "Hey!" he yelled in her direction. "That's too many goddamn shrimp in that motherfucker!"

Oh Jesus, this dude is counting shrimp!

"You understand, nigga?"

No, I have no idea what the fuck you're talking about with the shrimp, but I nodded my head. However, it soon became clear to me that, whatever else you might want to say about him, Michael Williams understood a Black audience. He knew that you had to come real strong to win them over.

He kept going, trying to give me more advice, but at some point I was thinking, *Okay, that's enough.* Maybe it was how cocky I was back then, but I always seemed to be filled with confidence—even when the confidence was totally unjustified. Time to justify it.

As I sat there watching, Robin Harris started introducing me.

"Okay, this next motherfucker coming to the stage, you ain't never seen him on TV. Matter of fact, he ain't never gonna be on TV. I take it back. He be on TV—he got a TV in the house. A little bitty-ass TV with just a mouth on the motherfucker, with an extension cord running all the way to the goddamn gas station. Give it up for a real good friend of mine—aw, fuck it, come on, motherfucker!"

I got onstage and pulled the first half of my act out my ass.

"Give it up for Robin Harris," I said. "He's having a tough day, to say the least. I knew Robin was trippin' because when I called up here to get my spot, he's the one that answered the phone."

Then I did a dead-on accurate impersonation of Robin—after just seeing him for the first time that night. "Hello? Who the fuck is this?" I said in Robin's voice. I did fifteen minutes in Robin's voice and the crowd was going insane. It wouldn't be an exaggeration to say that Robin Harris at the

Regency West was funnier than Richard Pryor and Eddie Murphy put together. It was his world and he totally dominated every aspect of it. To have this young kid up there with a dried-up Jheri curl, wearing an old-ass leather jacket from Terrell, doing Robin Harris was unthinkable. No one ever touched Robin. But here I was, daring to take him on. I was the baby petting the pit bull, totally oblivious to the danger.

After doing Harris, I went into my act, trotting out some of the stuff I had been working on—Black comedy standards, like the differences between Black people and white people.

"When you go to white weddings, the song at the beginning is right to the point: *Today is our wedding day, forever you will be mine. I will always love you, till the end of time.* Married. Black weddings? The song alone is forty-five minutes. Same song, but we do it like this: *Today, ay-ay-ay-ay-ay, yeah, yeah, is our wedding day-ay-ay-ay-ay . . .* You get the point. Black people, white people—there's not one that's better. It just has to do with the heart. The average white man's heart beats like this: *boom boom, boom boom, boom boom.* While the average Black man's heart beats like this . . ."

I did the human beatbox to imitate a Black man's heartbeat—and the crowd went crazy. But then I furthered the joke: "Ladies. That's why you have a choice when it comes to making love. Would you rather make love to someone like this?" I did the monotone white heartbeat: *boom boom, boom boom, boom boom*. "Or would you rather make love like this?" And then I did the Black heartbeat, sounding like a human beatbox. As I grinded my hips, those ladies in the front row went crazy. I knew I had them—so I furthered the joke again. As I was doing the beatbox, I said, "Turn over," and I changed up the beat to something faster.

Now everybody was up, as if they were watching *Def Comedy Jam*. Then I went even further: "Grab your ankles," I said. And I changed up the beat once more, to something that sounded like electronic dance music.

"Thank you. My name is Eric Bishop." I dropped the mic and walked off the stage. The crowd ate it up, jumping to their feet for a standing ovation.

I looked out into the audience and saw Harvey Fuqua, who showed up just in time to see me, nodding and staring at me with an expression on his face that said, *Damn, this motherfucker really is funny.* Robi Reed had a look in her eye, too, like, *Yo, this guy can be something.* But I wasn't even concerned about them. I wanted to get back to the table where those girls were sitting. Not that I wanted to get at them—I just wanted their opinion. I'm always checking for the toughest critic in the crowd. Speaking of tough critics, when Robin Harris came back to the stage, I was fully prepared for him to roast my ass. And so was the crowd. But I guess he must have seen what everybody else was seeing; he simply said, "*Shiiiit*, that's a funny muthafucka there! You need to get that Jheri curl fixed though."

When I sat back at the table, one of the pretty girls asked me, "You want a drink?"

"Are you hungry?" another one said.

"Why didn't you tell us you was a comic?" they asked.

I shrugged. "I tried to tell y'all I was the shit. Y'all didn't want to hear me."

That's LA. If you on, the ladies will give you attention. And if you ain't, well, you'll be counting how many shrimp are in the basket while you serve drinks.

Michael came to get me and dragged me in the back. He pulled out a greasy contract and said, "Sign right here." We were standing next to the fryer where they make the shrimp.

"Nah, I ain't signing," I said.

But I did sign with Robi Reed, who became my manager. She happened to be casting a show called *Roc*, starring Charles S. Dutton and Ella Joyce. I went in for an audition and wound up getting the part. But when it came time to shoot the pilot, my part wasn't included. That was a tough break for me because I had told everybody back in Terrell that I was going to be on TV. When the show aired and I was nowhere to be found, everybody thought I was lying, like maybe I was on drugs out there in California and hallucinating.

Despite that initial disappointment, I did end up getting cast in a few roles here and there that didn't get cut, and Eric Bishop became Jamie Foxx (I'll get to that a bit later). And the people that affected me along that journey always stuck with me. Harvey helped me out for many years, Michael Williams also became a bit of a mentor to me (sometimes with useful, unconventional advice). Although Robin Harris and I never became close, him tipping his hat to me at the comedy club propelled my confidence. So even though my priority is always Corinne and Anelise, when I meet their friends, I remember that I'm a distant part of their village too. Sure, I'm not raising these kids, but I still try to be encouraging and interested.

So when your kids bring home dumbass friends, remember you're part of their village. There's more than enough love to go around for everyone.

GIVE IT UP FOR
NOT GIVING IT UP

In this world, you are gonna hear "*No*" a lot. Doesn't matter what life path you take. You wanna be a doctor, odds are you'll be turned down from a few medical schools. You wanna be a baker, there's gonna be haters who don't like your muffins. Every person deals with a ton of rejection, but nothing compares to how much rejection you face when you go into entertainment. You can't get every role and you'll never be the best at everything. One thing I was never the best at—dance.

I was attending USIU in San Diego and I was disturbed when I saw one of the courses on my schedule: dance. Sure, I would drop it like it's hot at the club, but professional dancing?! That included tights, ballet shoes and the dreaded dance belt. For those wondering what a dance belt is, imagine a jock with one strap. Where does that one strap go? #ThongThongThongThongThong. *Aw, hell no!* When I walked into my mandatory ballet class with boxer shorts over sweatpants and Converse sneakers, the instructor immediately rushed over to me.

"What is this? Why don't you have your uniform?" *Because I'm not wearing a fucking thong,* I wanted to say. But instead I went with, "I don't have one."

He threw up his hands in disbelief but still agreed to see me dance. When he saw me step all over the toes (literally) of some of the most talented ballet dancers in the country, he yelled out, more than once, "Bishop, you're killing my students!"

After a few days of being the black bull in the ballet class, I could've given up—dropped the class or accepted an F—but I don't quit. Instead, I thought about what could benefit my dance teacher and brokered a deal with him.

"Listen. I'm not good at this," I said. "But you know what I *am* good at? Playing the piano. Why don't I play for your students instead of breaking their feet? Could I get a passing grade for that?"

He was skeptical at first. How could someone so ungraceful at dance be any good at piano? Well, I showed him, and next thing you know I was playing for *all* the ballet classes. Not only did I get credit, they also paid me seventeen dollars an hour. I was ballin'. I saved enough money to buy a car, a Triumph TR7, but you already know about how I lost that car.

Getting creative instead of giving up is one of the most important traits on the path to success— and one I'm trying on a daily basis to instill in my daughters. But this wasn't even an example of me getting a direct, hard "no." Here's a time the door got fucking shut in my face and I got it back open:

Early in my career, I was trying to get a part in the Oliver Stone movie *Any Given Sunday*. I hadn't been in any major movies yet, but that felt like the path I needed to be on. See, even though I had success with *In Living Color*, and *The Jamie Foxx Show* was going well, I still didn't feel like I had forged my own lane in comedy. Martin Lawrence, Eddie Murphy and Chris Rock were taking up all the air in the room. All the funny I tried to do was received by people as imitating or stealing. That's just an unfortunate fact of how the entertainment industry works: You can't have too many big Black acts at the same time. For comedy, in the '60s it was Redd Foxx; the '70s was Richard Pryor; the '80s was Eddie Murphy. Now in the '90s there was an opportunity for more than one of us to eat, but if you didn't find your slot it looked like you were mimicking somebody. I knew I was doing my own shit, but all these voices were in my head and I started to listen...Was I less funny or less talented than these peers of mine?

I had a reading for a prominent Black producer for the movie *How to Be a Player* that I'll never forget. While I was doing my comedy shtick, the producer was off to the side doing his own commentary.

I did a few lines and then I heard him say, "Oh, that's Martin." I did a few more and heard, "That's Chris. Chris Rock." Finally, I stopped. "Yo, money. What's up?" I said.

He was a bit taken aback. "No, no. I'm just saying, you sounded for a second like you were doing Eddie Murphy. The whole time you were talking I was like, 'Okay, this is Eddie Murphy.' And then I thought, 'That's Martin.' I'm sorry, was that disrespectful?" Yeah dude, it's pretty disrespectful!

When I left the room, I was pissed, wondering what the fuck this big producer was doing in the movie industry anyway. But he was the big boss, so he had final say. I never forgot that day, how I walked away feeling like I didn't have a spot. That's probably one of the moments in my life where I doubted myself the most. It's one thing if white people grouped a bunch of us Black comics together...but a *brother?!*

As it turned out, the timing couldn't have been better, because shortly after, I got a call from my manager saying they wanted me to go in and read for

Oliver Stone for a movie called *Any Given Sunday*. That was a huge deal; I was excited about it. This wasn't some guy dipping his toes in the movie industry. This guy made *Platoon*! *Natural Born Killers*! *Talk Radio*! Okay, full disclosure, I've never seen *Talk Radio*—but he still made that movie!

It just clicked in my head. Okay, so if "comedy" is my "dance," maybe "dramatic acting" is my "piano playing"? I knew the metaphor didn't make perfect sense because I was way fucking better at comedy than I've ever been at dance. But the point remains: I wasn't gonna let the entertainment industry shut me out. I was gonna get a big role in a major fucking movie.

However, when I read for Oliver, it quickly looked like that was going to turn into another nightmare. I never got acting lessons like I did piano lessons. Everything I knew about performing, I learned by doing. And by the nature of stand-up and television, that doing happened in front of a live audience. And that couldn't be more different than film acting. See, when you're doing comedy in front of an audience, you play off their energy. They laugh, you go bigger. Sitcoms are kind of like performing a live play: You go big to make sure even the people in the back row are falling out their seats laughing. Acting for the movie camera is the opposite. They're gonna get you in a close-up, which means your face will take up the entire movie screen (or TV screen or phone screen, depending where someone's watching). And when the audience can see every subtle movement your face makes...Less Is More. But I didn't know that back then, so when I read, I was too loud. I was a TV actor, so I was used to being over-the-top, extra emotive.

"Haha! Yeah! What it be, man?!" I delivered way, way louder than Oliver could've possibly envisioned when writing the script.

Oliver stopped me. "What are you doing?" he asked.

"Um, I'm just trying to emote, Oliver Stone."

He stared at me and told me to my face, "You're no good." Now, most people in Hollywood play the game of being nice to your face, but this guy had more Oscars than balls and bigger balls than almost anyone I've ever met. I mean, he made *JFK*, a movie about how the CIA murdered the president. If he wasn't scared of the CIA, he sure as hell wasn't scared of me.

"Anyway, nice to meet you," he said, and I was out the door. And as soon as I closed the door, I heard him say to his assistant: "Jamie Foxx, stuck in television."

I was really upset. I called my people and went off. "Man, fuck this motherfucker! I don't give a fuck what movies he did, man. I'm Jamie Foxx!" Tough pill to swallow. I was in the fourth season of a television show that was named after me. I thought I was the shit. But in the Hollywood hierarchy, which had a famous multiple Academy Award–winning director like Oliver Stone sitting astride the top, I was squirming somewhere in the middle of the totem pole.

I originally read for the part of Julian Washington that LL Cool J wound up playing in the movie. They asked me to come back and read for the part of the agent. I should probably give props to my own agent, who got me back into that room. But Stone still didn't like me.

"Well, you're just no good at that either," he told me when I was done.

When I walked out of the room, I said under my breath, "Fuck it." I thought it was over. It's one thing to blow an audition in a humiliating way but to be brought back for another role...and rejected as harshly? Damn! I did my best to put Oliver Stone out of my mind, but we got a very surprising call from Oliver's casting agent.

"You're not going to believe this, but Oliver Stone wants you in the movie as the agent," she told me.

"Man, fuck that motherfucker!" I said. You ever think some girl is gonna turn you down so you make up in your mind you actually didn't like her? I thought this role would get pulled out from under my feet, so my impulse was to reject it first. But my agent calmed me down and convinced me to accept it. I would end up playing Willie Beamen (keep reading), and Willie's agent would eventually be played by Duane Martin, but at that moment, the part seemed like mine.

So I met up with Oliver Stone to discuss further, and when I went in, everything felt different. He seemed a lot chiller and I couldn't figure out why... until I smelled all the weed. *Ah, okay, Mr. Stone, you're more of a Mr. Stoner.*

But even though he was being cool, I still felt the need to let him know how I felt. Yes, maybe I could fake it through this meeting without mentioning it, but if we were making a movie together, it would come out anyway. I'm not about being phony, so I decided to tell him to his face.

"Hey man, you know, I really took offense at what you said," I said.

"Aw, relax," he said, waving his hand.

"No, I took offense, you know what I'm saying?" I said. "I take this shit seriously."

"Oh, shut up," he said. "You got the part. What do you want me to tell you? You never done movies before; now you're in a movie." Actually, I had done a couple of "Black" movies, but nothing even close to this big.

Then he got a bit more serious. "But I got a problem though."

"What's the problem?"

"I need somebody to play the lead role, the Willie Beamen role. Do you think you can do it?" he asked.

What the hell?! He tells me I'm terrible during two auditions for smaller parts. Then gives me a part. Then tells me he wants me to play the *lead* instead?! What was this guy smoking?! Wait, I already knew the answer to that. But then it started to dawn on me: Maybe this was Oliver Stone's method. Maybe if he truly thought I was terrible, he would've just politely said bye to me and I never would've heard from him again. Maybe he saw something in me and saw it was locked up behind ego and wanted to take me down a peg. Or maybe he was just an indecisive asshole. But whatever cat-and-mouse game he was playing with me, I wasn't gonna be the one to back down. So I said hell yeah.

He told me that Puff Daddy originally had the part, but they were running into problems. In 1999, Diddy was in the midst of his rise as a music and fashion mogul, running enormously successful enterprises in addition to recording himself after Biggie's death. I wasn't privy to the details of his discussions with Oliver, but I was a bit leery about stepping into a part that had already been given to Puff.

"Hey, listen, I don't want to step on anybody's

toes. I'm not that kind of dude," I said. "So you run whatever course you have to run with Puff or whatever. Once you've done that, just let me know. I'm here."

When they tied that up, I got the part. But Oliver still seemed to hate my acting. He would have me come in and read and read and read, to no avail. Now, most directors would give you a compliment sandwich where they'd start by saying something nice and then give you a small note to adjust your performance and then close the sandwich with another piece of nice. Not Oliver Stone.

"You're just fucking terrible, kid," he finally told me. "I can't tell these people this is your part. I can't show Warner Bros. this footage. I can't really make you the guy unless you get better. You suck at this. Stop doing that sitcom thing you're doing, whatever that, that shit is. This is movies. This is big! The screen is huge! You come out there with that, 'I'm Willie!' that shit is too much for people. Cut it out!"

He looked at me closely. "I gotta sell you to Warner Bros. They think you're that—what's that show you do? Your Jamie Foxx-whatever-it-is, that show—you do a TV show, right? Yeah, you're doing that thing. Well, this isn't that."

Man, I cannot tell you how frustrated and devastated I was by this point. I felt I was going to have the biggest opportunity of my career thus far taken away. And then I thought back to that dance class. If "dramatic acting" was my "dancing," what's my piano playing? And then I realized I was looking at it all wrong. Maybe I wasn't good at dance class, but I was totally fine dancing at the club. At the club, I wasn't overthinking my dance moves, I was just present with the music...and the ladies. Why was I overthinking playing a football player? I didn't need to make big acting choices for every line of dialogue. I really *was* a fucking football player. I was literally a quarterback. I passed for a few thousand yards in high school!

That's when it clicked. Whether or not Oliver Stone had given up on me by that point, I hadn't given up on me. I came up with the idea to shoot my own video, playing the part of Willie Beamen, and show Stone that I was more than just a guy who does sitcoms. So I grabbed a group of guys, put on my Dallas Cowboys helmet and we jumped in this dope Mercedes coupe I had just bought. We filmed ourselves like we were at training camp, playing football, running plays. Then we came up with this chant:

"My name is Willie," I said.

And my homies sang, "Wil-lie Bea-men!"

"I keep the ladies," I said.

"Creamin'!" they chanted.

"I keep the fans."

"Screamin'!"

"You know what they sayin'," I said.

"Willie Beamen!"

I just started being him, envisioning him as some kind of Deion Sanders character. I wasn't worried about lines, about acting. I just said, "Let me play football and y'all catch me on camera embodying this character." I gave the video to Oliver. That same day I got a call from him.

"Get back to the office right now!" he said. When I walked in, he came over and hugged me.

"You did it!" he said. "This is Willie Beamen."

He turned my video in to Warner Bros. and got the green light for me in the part. You can watch my video on the *Any Given Sunday* DVD, where it's included as one of the extras.

Tangentially, Oliver Stone also played a crucial role in another situation where I refused to hear no. I was about twenty episodes away from my 100th episode on *The Jamie Foxx Show*. A hundred episodes was an enormous benchmark because that meant the show could be sold into syndication, which would bring significant cash to everyone involved. As hard as I worked to get cast in *Any Given Sunday*, there was no guarantee that *Ali*, *Collateral* and *Ray* were coming after. I very vividly remembered growing up poor, so I *needed* this show to hit a hundred episodes to guarantee my existing daughter and any future daughters wouldn't ever experience that. We worked so hard to get the show on the air and even harder getting it to eighty episodes. It was *not* getting canceled before one hundred.

So I asked Oliver as a favor to come down to set. When this famous movie director walked onto the set of *The Jamie Foxx Show*, it threw everybody into a tizzy. They don't see movie dudes very often; TV people are in awe of movie people.

"What's going on?" Oliver said as he started walking around the set, checking out the setup. "How do you do this? Four cameras, wow. Man, that's taking up a lot of time. Just shoot a wide shot and go home."

Then he said very calmly, "So I hear you're canceling the star of my movie." He turned to look at the executives.

"If I'm putting him in the movie, why are you cutting him short on his show?"

You should've seen their faces. It looked like they crapped their pants. Remember, this is the three-time Oscar winner who isn't scared of the CIA.

"No, no, no, we're not doing that," one of them said, stumbling over his words. "Oh, Jamie, c'mon! Hahaha. I don't know who gave you that information. No, we were never going to do that."

Then he asked, "Um, can we get a picture for me

and the family?" Oliver graciously took a picture with him, and I just stared, knowing he never wanted a picture of me to show his family. But just like that, Oliver Stone elongated my TV show by a season and we got to our 100th episode. I decided that made us even for all the shit he put me through auditioning for his movie.

I've done my best to build this sort of confidence in my daughters. To never give up. To not take no for an answer. Clever-ass Corinne turned this around on me, of course. "But Dad, you always told me that no means no and guys should respect when I say no to them." Alright, damn, you got me! There are absolutely situations where no should mean "hell fucking no." So I'm glad I taught my daughters the importance of consent, but I also taught them to always believe in themselves, even when no one else does. However, there is no possible scenario where no one else does, because I always will.

GETTING TO THE PEARLY GATES

I grew up in Texas, so I don't even need to tell you that I was raised religiously. I could just say "I grew up in Texas" and you would know I'm probably Protestant. As a kid, I would blindly believe everything I was told, and I'm still a deep believer, but I began to question things when I was still in Terrell. Learning my dad was a Muslim was the first time I had to ask myself, "Well, *why* am I a Christian?" And I started to develop a jaded view of organized religion because of what I saw behind the pulpit while playing piano for the church. I remember having a revelation at age fourteen about how it all felt like a racket. I even confronted the pastor. Which, believe me, was one of the scariest things I ever had to do.

"How much does it cost to go to heaven—'cause Miss Odessa ain't got no money and I just saw her open her napkin to give her last dollar when I happen to know her lights ain't on at the house?" I was trembling asking him this. I knew he was just a man, but part of me thought he was like Santa Claus, keeping a list of who goes to heaven and who goes to the other place.

"Oh, we just going to keep raising money," he said, dismissing me. His casualness about it was even more upsetting than if he'd got mad at me.

I saw that when I played extra well, it made the congregation more eager to give their money, maybe their last dime. It was confusing because it made sense for show business—if you're a better musician, you'll have more of a chance to make money—but it didn't make sense for God. How much money did God need? I know he rested on the seventh day, but he could've used the eighth day to create enough Benjamins for himself that he didn't need Miss Odessa's bill money. I often felt guilty about this, but I never dared talk to my grandmother about it. She would've whupped my ass into the past century if I questioned the church.

As I got older, I learned that it was possible to keep two thoughts in your head at once. Sure, some aspects of the church confused me, but I do still have a very deep connection with God. I still attend church and pray daily. I never wanted to force that on my kids, but I also didn't want them to miss out on having a rewarding spiritual life. Not to mention maybe missing out on going to heaven. How awkward would it be when I get to heaven and am bragging to Jimi Hendrix or Richard Pryor about my kids and they ask where they are and I'm like, "Oh, they're burning in hell for eternity."

So I took my daughters to church when they were little, but as they've gotten older, I've given them a lot of room to explore their own spirituality—to see what feels comfortable to them—giving them more options than I had. When Corinne was thirteen, we did a segment on my Sirius XM show, *The Foxxhole*, about LGBTQ rights. This was thirteen years ago, so many of the issues weren't as prominent as they are today. Even though the show was wrapped in comedy, we got quite serious that day. I had invited Corinne and her friends to the studio, so they were there taking it all in. When we got back in the limo, I asked them, "So, what's you guys' take on this?"

"Dad, can I speak freely?" Corinne asked.

My eyes widened. *Oh damn.* But I said, "Sure."

"Grown people make everything a spectacle," she said. "All grown people do is talk about people that are different."

"You know, we don't care at all," one of her male friends chimed in.

And when we got to the topic of religion . . . "That's the other thing," he said. "All you guys keep talking about who's got the best way to go to heaven. It really doesn't make sense to us. That's why we sort of like don't get involved. Because if one person says they're Baptist and another person says they're Catholic, then all of a sudden you guys got beef. And we're like, all grown people do is argue and talk about who's different."

I sat back, kinda blown away. I don't know if this was their generation or their liberal California upbringing, but they were making a lot of sense—it was still somewhat new to me to not discuss religion in black-and-white terms. Corinne and her friends were telling me they weren't here for the choosing sides, for the thinking that says you must be part of this particular religious entity to go to heaven instead of hell. Despite Corinne never being that interested in religion, she always had a strong moral code. It's always been a part of who she is, and as a result, she has grown up to be one of the nicest people on the planet.

Anelise was different from her sister in the sense that since an early age she has been fascinated by religion and has been curious about investigating different religions and heritages. She longs to visit Egypt because she's infatuated with the tombs and King Tut and all of that. So I guess she's a pagan. To counterbalance the paganism, I had her learn all the books of the Bible. Back in Terrell, it was a thing— when you got to age four, you had to memorize all the titles. I don't know why we did it—it's not like we expected to end up at the Pearly Gates with St. Peter giving us a pop quiz. Amazingly, I still have them memorized, almost a half century later. I had forgotten about the tradition until I was hanging with my boy Gilbert, my best friend from Texas. He came to my house with his four-year-old twin sons.

"You on your Bible game, dog?" he asked me. Then he looked at his boys. "Hit it!" he said. Those boys went in: "Genesis, Exodus, Leviticus, Numbers, Deuteronomy, Joshua, Judges…"

Then he said, "Where your daughter at? She know 'em, dog?"

At the time Anelise was only three, so we got a pass. But I told her, "Look, you got to understand the tradition. When you turn four you got to know the books of the Bible." And she said she would before she hit three and a half. So we quietly started working on it. The next time I saw Gil, I said, "Anelise, hit it!" And she smoothly reeled off all the books of the Old Testament.

"Ohhh!" Gil said, impressed. I beamed, so proud of her. She slipped in a few books that weren't in the Bible, like King David and the Prisoner of Azkaban, but she hit the correct ones too. In 2012, she chanted the books of the Bible again on cue from the stage at the Democratic National Convention in Charlotte, and the crowd went wild. I'm not gonna say that's *why* Obama got reelected, but it didn't hurt him!

Obviously the book names aren't the important part of the Bible. The book of Habakkuk could be named the book of Spaghetti and Meatballs and it'll still be full of lessons about why you shouldn't do evil. So I made sure that we read the words in them as well. I told both of my girls: Even if you don't believe all the stories literally, if you listen to them they are providing you with tools on how to be a conscious, responsible, moral person. How to treat your fellow man. How to live your life, how to prioritize your spirituality.

I came from a very strong, strict background when it came to religion, but I knew that rigid way wasn't the way in for them. I wanted their spirituality to be an open-ended conversation. Faith is an ever-growing thing, so sometimes I even learn from my daughters. One time, Anelise asked me if I would commit murder if I somehow knew for a fact God didn't exist. I thought about her question seriously and said no, of course I wouldn't murder someone. So did I learn not to murder from the Bible? Or from my grandparents? Or did I just grow up in society innately knowing killing is bad? I still believe spirituality should be a huge part of my life and my daughter's lives, but maybe it's not needed to prevent you from stabbing someone. And don't get me started on people who commit violence in the name of God.

Of course, the flipside of having an open dialogue with your children about God is sometimes they turn the table on you.

"Anelise, where's God?" I once asked her, as she sat in her car seat in the back. She was probably eight or so. A big part of what I wanted to instill in her about faith is that God doesn't live at church, God is everywhere.

"Right here," she said, putting her hand on her chest. *That's right, baby girl. God is always in your heart.* Then she added something new:

"But the Devil's here sometime too," she said. I almost wrecked the car.

"Whaaaat?" I said, looking at her in the rearview mirror.

"There is a Devil, right?" she said, as I looked closely to make sure the Devil wasn't sitting in the back seat with her.

"Yeah," I said. But I didn't know what to do with her declaration. *Why is my child talking about the Devil being in her heart? Do I need a kindergarten exorcist?*

But she was right! If living free of sin was the

easiest thing in the world, we wouldn't need Jesus Christ to die for our sins. And if Jesus Christ didn't die for our sins, we wouldn't have Easter eggs! As much as I didn't love the visual of Satan himself being within my daughter, she was right that the Devil is around and tempting us. So maybe I'm not the world's greatest evangelist—I ain't got a private jumbo jet like Creflo Dollar—but clearly I was doing something right.

Another thing I always have to remember is that kids think their parents are uncool. It doesn't matter if you're literally Jamie Foxx who made a hit song with Kanye West, when you're singing along to the radio, you're probably embarrassing your daughters. So when you introduce religion to your kids, just make sure you don't hammer it so hard that they label it as some uncool thing parents are into, close the door to any relationship with God and burn in you-know-where forever.

NEW DAD

When it came time for Corinne to start dating, I'll admit that I had a hard time figuring out where to erect the barriers. I don't even like using the words "hard" or "erect" in the same sentence as my daughter. Things were so different from when I was a teenager. For example, if I wanted to holla at a girl, I had to physically holla at her or call her house, where her daddy was bound to pick up. In Corinne's case, I didn't have the same opportunity to intercept phone calls. I would see her phone light up and have no idea who the hell was texting her.

I had to make things up as I went along since I didn't have a lot of other dads of girls her age to compare notes with. At school events, the other parents seem to see only the public version of me, the entertainer who told funny stories on *Jimmy Kimmel*, not some guy who would struggle to make polite, awkward small talk with some boy who's trying to date my daughter even though I know I can easily throw his ass through the wall. I don't want to be the Hollywood guy at PTA meetings though. Can we just gossip about our kids' teachers instead of y'all asking me about celebrity gossip? Honestly, these parents have got more celebrity dirt than I do. One of them knew about a movie role I was getting before I did! I called up my agent like, "I'm doing an Edgar Wright movie?" and he was all "Yeah, didn't you see it on *Deadline*?" But at the end of the day, I'm struggling with the same stuff as these parents and figuring out how to navigate it all.

That said, I'm not above throwing a little bit of Hollywood into my parenting methods. One time, Corinne was bringing a guy by the crib while I was home. That day I happened to have a guest . . . Snoop Dogg. This opportunity I just couldn't resist. I pointed the guy out to Snoop Dogg and told him to shake him up. When Corinne left the room, it went over like that scene from *Bad Boys*. "Hey, what up, nephew?" Snoop Dogg came at him, "You understand what's going on right now?" Fortunately, this guy took it well, which was a good sign. Clearly, no punk kid wants both Jamie Foxx and Snoop

Dogg on his ass if he's messing up, so the fact that he wasn't nervous made me think he wasn't messing up. When Corinne came back, we dropped the tough act and started pretending everyone was best friends—Snoop even took a few selfies with him. I don't think the guy ever told Corinne that we messed with him or she would've given me a mouthful. And Snoop would've taken her side.

So how strict or lax was I going to be when it came to my daughters dating? Hollywood isn't exactly known for its stern parenting practices; I didn't want to be as laissez-faire as the parents I saw around me. "Oh, our darling child just got their second DUI? Let's let the lawyers handle that and get him a brand-new BMW to replace the one he wrecked." But I knew what could happen when you go too far in the other direction and your kids decide that they need to break out of jail in a big way. I needed to figure out what keeping Texas with me looked like in this situation.

So being an Old-School Dad wasn't gonna cut it, and being an LA No-Dad was a no go, so I came up with a new concoction known as... "New Dad." New Dad was a little more progressive and forward thinking, not because he worried about his daughter less but because he worried about her in a smarter way. New Dad attacked parenting challenges in a much different way than Old-School Dad. When talking to a daughter about to begin dating, Old-School Dad might say something like, "You know, just find somebody who's gonna treat you right," and leave it at that. New Dad is gonna roll up his sleeves and get in there. "Let me tell you what they tryna do—they tryna hit it." And then New Dad is gonna teach her about condoms. Not to *encourage* sex, but New Dad knows, odds are he won't be able to prevent sex, and New Dad ain't about to become New Granddad.

I was convinced that New Dad was the way to go—which would be a very different way of approaching sexuality than I got when I was growing up in Terrell. It's better for my kids to get this sensitive info from me, New Dad, than from the idiots on the streets like I did. When I think back to my own sex education, all I can do is shake my damn head. I learned way too much from two older brothers in my neighborhood named Mitchell and Aaron. They were about ten years older than me and I thought they were the flyest dudes in Texas. They had a dirt basketball court in their yard, so we all would spend time over there playing—or at least waiting for the older guys to give us a chance to take some shots. Often during their games, the conversation would drift to girls and sex. One day when I was about ten, they started talking shit. Mitchell said Jeanette from up the street had let him "go the whole nine." We all hooted in response.

Mitchell looked at me quizzically and said, "Severi-tis, you don't know what that mean."

I should interject that Mitchell for some reason had given me the nickname Severitis. I have no idea what it means or where it came from—this was the '70s, during the era of Parliament-Funkadelic, so everybody was getting outlandish nicknames. I could sit here for half the day and not be able to trace the origins of that damn name. I never bothered to ask Mitchell what it meant; I was just grateful that he noticed me enough to bother granting me any nickname. Mitchell was cool, all the girls liked him, his family had money and he seemed like a man about the world. I didn't care what he called me. His parents owned a car wash—to my mind, he and Aaron were rich. Certainly, they weren't on the free lunch like I was. I think Mitchell eventually became a city councilman.

I think I did know what Mitchell meant, but I was embarrassed to break it down in front of them. Aaron, who was holding the basketball, shirtless, interjected.

"Oh, you know what that is, little man. It's when you do like this and get up in there." Aaron felt the need to thrust his hips to demonstrate.

"Ohhhh!!" they all exclaimed.

"Yeah, that's what I do," Aaron continued. "You spit off in there."

You spit in it? I didn't know what that meant. I don't think my young cohorts did either, because one of them said, "Why y'all spittin'?" The older guys laughed until their bellies hurt.

A few years later, my sexual escapades found their way into my house in a most unpleasant scene. I had already been playing piano for the church for a couple of years, messing around with older church girls. One morning when I was fifteen, my grandfather burst into the house when I was eating breakfast. His face was dripping with outrage.

"Boy, what's all that calm doing in the seats?"

My eyes widened and I turned into Eddie Haskell from *Leave It to Beaver*.

"Grandfather, whatsoever do you mean?"

"You know what the fuck I mean, nigga! What's the calm doing in the seats?"

I started stammering.

"You had a girl in there!" he said. "There's calm on the seat. I know it's calm."

"Are you saying 'calm'?" I asked—though I knew damn well what he was saying.

"Calm, nigga!"

He grabbed me by my shirt and literally dragged me out to his car. He had an enormous LTD Crown Victoria with two big bucket seats that might as well have been a split-level condo to my horny fifteen-year-old eyes. I had taken an older girl from church out in the car the night before, not long after I had gotten my provisional license. Some stuff definitely happened in there, but I was certain I had been real slick about it.

My grandfather opened the car door, palmed my head and pushed it down toward the back seat, like he was disciplining a dog after it shit in the house.

"That ain't no goddamn calm on the seat?!" he said. Mind you, my grandfather had never uttered a word to me about sex. That made the moment especially torturous.

"No, it ain't!" I said, squealing like a pig.

Then he twisted my head around and said, "Then what the fuck is them footprints doing up in the ceiling?! You clean this goddamn car!"

One day, about a year after LTD-gate, my grandmother looked over at me and asked a question.

"Eric, you hear about these girls putting the things in their mouth?"

I felt my heart skip several beats. Nooo, that could not be what she was asking me.

"Granny, what you talkin' about?" I asked innocently, summoning my early acting skills.

"They say they put they mouths on the peepee," she said.

Yep. That's where she was going.

"Granny, I don't know what you talking about."

"You know what I'm talking about! They say that

the girl go down on they knees and put the peepee in their mouth. Do girls do that?"

I felt my neck get real hot. *What the hell?*

"Granny, I've never heard of that before."

"I say that's nasty," she said. "Put the peepee in the mouth. I ain't never heard nothing like that."

I wanted to dive through the closest window, whether it was open or not. But as I got older and thought back to that conversation, I got sad for my grandfather, for all the implications. Enough said. (Bulging-eyes emoji)

That was my sex education. I felt like I should at least improve upon that when I talked to my own kids. I wanted my approach to be just a little bit more progressive. And with the access modern kids have to every kind of porn imaginable right there in their hands, it's essential we get into it as early as possible. In my generation we might have had to sneak and reach under our father's mattress to get to the dirty magazine. Shit, if that stuff was right there on a device I carried in my pocket, I might have never left my room. Even if it's uncomfortable, New Dad needs to wade in there and be vocal, because they're going to see it. We can't fool ourselves into thinking they won't. I've noticed that whenever I pick up my daughter's phone, all of her history will be cleared. *Hmmm.*

"Anelise, why you kill your history?" I asked her

one day. "Why you ain't got no history on your phone?"

She looked at me, wide-eyed and silent. Note to parents who know how to act: Don't teach your kids how to do it too early, you're just teaching them how to lie. Now I knew something was up.

So, one day I walked into the room and quickly asked her, "What you lookin' at on your phone?!"

Her eyes turned into saucers. Busted!

I said, "You gotta tell me. It's gonna be worse if you don't tell me."

Anelise almost has a panic attack if she's caught doing something wrong; she hates to be in trouble. This time, I thought she was going to have a seizure.

"I-I-I don't want to show you," she said. "I don't want to show you."

"No, get yourself together, but you gonna show me, because this is learning. It's worse if you don't show me, but you have to show me what it is."

She went to look for it, because she had tried to delete it. While she was looking, I was about to have a panic attack of my own. *My God, what is it? The girl is about to faint—what the hell could this be?* The first thing I saw was a cartoon, and my mind went to the worst place...I know the Japanese be putting out *dirty anime*. But very quickly I realized it was basically a Disney cartoon that somebody had altered and overdubbed with curse words. I whispered to myself, "Thank you, Jesus." I was relieved, but I had to do some acting and express outrage. If this is what she thought was *real bad*, I needed her to *keep* thinking this is real bad.

"Now, you know, we don't do this," I said. "You don't ever do this again, you understand what I'm saying?"

But even if she was doing something really bad, as a parent—especially as New Dad—it's always important to keep a level head and keep things in a perspective of how much worse things could get. And life often hits you with hard reminders of that.

A dear friend of mine lost his son in 2019. It hit me hard. I have been friends with this dude for nearly three decades, so I saw his boy grow up into a man. But my friend, who is also a comedian, never told us the truth about how many kids he has. At the funeral, his kids were coming from everywhere to give heart-felt speeches about their brother. Each time another kid went to the mic, we'd all be looking around asking each other, "Whoa, another one?"

When one of his daughters, who clearly had her dad's gift for comic timing, went to the mic, she said, "I'm one of my father's many daughters." The whole place went up in flames; we were all cracking up, a sorely needed bit of comic relief.

Then my friend went up and grabbed the mic.

"Okay, that's enough. Okay. Y'all not gonna be sitting here clowning me. I have some kids. Yes, I have some kids."

He literally did about two minutes of stand-up at his son's funeral—and it was beautiful. It was cleansing. "Look, man, I was in the streets," he said. "But I love all my kids. I love y'all." And he started naming them. He thought he was done because he couldn't remember any more. "Did I forget anybody?" he asked. And five hands shot up in the air.

A few days after the funeral, I was sitting in my house with Anelise and two of her young cousins, one thirteen and the other seventeen. The father of one of the cousins was there as well. I was recounting for them the scene from the funeral.

"The funny thing about my friend was that when we were on the road, he always had condoms," I said. I was enjoying the chuckle, but then I remembered my audience. "Y'all know about condoms, right? Come on, be honest."

They shrugged. One of them said, "We saw them in your room."

When I'm not there, they're always in my room, combing through my shit like they're searching for blood diamonds. My niece's father and I decided to give them a very brief primer on condoms. Okay, here we go. It's one thing to decide you'll be honest with your kids about sex, but it's another to put together sentences and say it to their little innocent faces. It is never easy to look right at your daughter and say "penis." Then say the "penis" makes "ejaculate," which the "condom" catches. I am even cringing typing this! But you gotta keep a straight face. You don't want them having some sort of fucked-up mental relationship with sex and be in therapy the rest of their lives. "When I was a little girl, my dad looked scared when he said 'ejaculate,' and now I can't have sex without crying."

When we were done with the talk, there were no follow-up questions. Just silence. By the looks on their faces, they would have been okay if they all could have melted and sunk down through the floorboards. That's New Dad for ya. He's honest about sex and now it's not some wild, alluring, mysterious thing.

I also had a prime opportunity to trot out New Dad with Corinne. We were filming *Django Unchained* in Louisiana, at an actual former sugarcane plantation, so I decided it would be an educational experience for my family to come to the set. I don't know what I expected—on the call sheet they had grips and gaffers, not historical experts ready to give families tours of the set. Quentin Tarantino is a genius, but his manipulation of historical accuracy is partly what he's known for. I mean this motherfucker literally killed Hitler in his previous movie!

(Sorry for the spoiler but that movie's been out for over a decade.)

Corinne showed up shortly after her eighteenth birthday in early 2012. Once she got there, she looked around at all the stars in the movie, including Leonardo, the great Samuel L. Jackson, Kerry Washington and Christoph Waltz, and she just couldn't understand what I was doing there.

"Dad, why'd they pick you?" she asked. I looked at her. The girl was serious. She had sat right there next to me when I won the Academy Award in 2005, seven years earlier. Maybe she thought the Academy had made a mistake.

Corinne seemed to really enjoy herself that day on set, taking pictures with the other stars and observing the magic of filmmaking at the hands of Tarantino, one of the best to ever do it. She was still in denial about wanting to pursue acting full time, but I saw her in video village, mouthing along with the words to the scene.

Oh, I forgot to mention: Corinne showed up... with her boyfriend. Like many fathers of daughters, the presence of a boyfriend puts me on immediate high alert. I want to be courteous and gracious, but a part of me also wants to punch him in the throat for no reason. Especially after it got to evening time and we all retired to the house I was staying at. "Where are we sleeping?"

Corinne asked. *WE?! As in where are you AND your boyfriend sleeping?!*

Corinne hadn't introduced me to many of her boyfriends, and I was all ready to sink into Old Dad. Thank God, I was able to take a deep breath instead, put on my New Dad hat and look at the situation as a realist. Nothing I do or say is going to change the likelihood that my lovely daughter will become involved with boys. How can New Dad finesse this and make it work for everybody involved? This was a prime opportunity for New Dad tactics.

"Okay," I said, "this is what's going to happen. I know what you guys are going to do—you're gonna respect me. So I'm going to let you sleep in the same bedroom. Okay? You see, I'm trying something new."

Corinne had no idea what I was talking about— and didn't care. She just wanted to go to sleep. So she headed to the bedroom. Her boyfriend started to follow her, but I grabbed him by the arm before he left the room.

"Listen!" I said in a stage whisper. "Don't fuck me up!"

He looked at me with a mix of fear and confusion.

"What do you mean?" What did I mean? Did I have to have the birds-and-bees talk with this fool, too?!

"You know exactly what I mean," I said. "You can

do anything when I'm not around or whatever." I thought about how that sounded. "Well, I'm not saying you could do *anything*, but I'm just saying, you gotta respect me. Don't fuck me up. You know what I'm saying?"

He stared at me and nodded.

"Yeah, I got you," he said.

Off he went, to join Corinne in the bedroom. I was thinking, *Yeah, this is going to work, because I'm New Dad, remember.*

I went to one of the other bedrooms, where Anelise and her mom were about to go to sleep.

"What are you doing?" Kristin asked me, all kinds of judgment in her voice.

"What do you mean, what am I doing?"

"You're going to let your daughter be in the same bedroom with a guy?" she said. "Alone?"

"Yeah," I said. "Because I'm New Dad. I know what I'm doing. I'm basically taking the adventure out of it, you know what I'm saying? I'm taking the sneakiness out of it. They know not to disrespect me because I'm basically taking all of the hype and adrenaline out of sneaking around."

She rolled her eyes. "Well, whatever," she said. "You won't be doing that with our daughter."

"Nah, I got this," I said. I was thinking, *She's Old Mom. I'm New Dad.*

I went to my room and lay my head down on

the pillow. Eleven p.m., I was so proud of myself. Midnight, doubts started creeping in. One a.m., I realized I wasn't going to be able to fall asleep. Two a.m., my mind was racing like crazy—I was having flashbacks to myself as a teenager. When I turned sixteen, my hips started to gyrate uncontrollably. That's how horny I was, walking around looking like I was auditioning for a Magic Mike show (shout-out to my boy Channing Tatum). That image stuck in my head as I thought about my baby girl in the room with that eighteen-year-old boy. Three a.m., it dawned on me: I let my daughter and some *guy* share a bedroom!

Four a.m., New Dad had a straight-up anxiety attack. I jumped out of the bed and went to Kristin's room.

"Listen, I got to find out," I said. "I got to go in there."

She sat up slowly, wondering what the hell I was talking about.

"What?"

"I got to go in there," I repeated.

"What are you gonna do?"

"I don't know," I said, shrugging my shoulders. "I'll figure it out."

I left that room and slowly crept over to their bedroom. My heart was lodged firmly in my throat, and my stomach was filled with butterflies—butterflies that were hoping I wasn't about to catch any foolish-ness. What in the world was I doing? I thought, *You dumb motherfucker, this could be a moment that will scar both you and your daughter for life.*

I did one of those quick knocks and pushed open the door, like the cleaning lady at the hotel who barges in and catches you butt naked. I didn't want to give them time to stop whatever they were doing. If anything was happening, it was about to be murder on the dance floor.

When I stepped into the room, it took me a second to focus my eyes. *Busted*, I thought. They were both in bed together! But then, when my brain caught up with my eyes, I realized the boyfriend was laying on top of the covers with his clothes on sleeping in the op-posite direction while Corinne was snug underneath the covers, both of them sound asleep. It was even more PG than the cartoon Anelise was watching.

Was New Dad right? Was I dead-on in my ana-lysis? I have no idea. All I know is that my daughter is awesome. Corinne still has no idea that I snuck into their room—until she reads the story on this page. I apologize, baby girl. New Dad panicked for a second.

After being greeted with that heartwarming sight, I crept back into Kristin's room. She had already gone back to sleep, so I shook her awake.

"Get up!" I said.

"What?" she said.

"You get up. I will show you right now. I told you I'm New Dad. New Dad works."

Like a proud peacock, I led her to Corinne's room and pushed the door ajar. She looked at me with a smirk that said, *Whatever, New Dad—don't try that shit with Anelise.*

At the end of the day, New Dad, Old Dad, Middle Dad, Whatever-the-Fuck Dad...Dads are dads and you're gonna worry about your kids. No matter which tactics you deploy, you're always gonna second-guess and wonder if you're doing the right thing. I guess my piece of advice is to be flexible and recalibrate. When I thought New Dad wasn't working, I recalibrated and busted into Corinne's room, and when I thought Dad Who Busts into Rooms wasn't working, I recalibrated and snuck outta there with my tail between my legs. The most important thing is just to keep doing your best.

So if you're getting to the end of this chapter and you're wondering, "Did this dude seriously just spend a whole chapter telling me about how to be a New Dad and then wrap it up by shrugging his shoulders and telling me there isn't really one answer and to keep doing my best?" Yes. Next chapter.

THE TALE OF TWO PARTIES

In 2012, I had the overly ambitious idea to celebrate New Year's Eve in Australia with Anelise and a bunch of my friends and family, then fly back to Las Vegas and celebrate it all over again with teenage Corinne and her friends. Anelise was only four at the time, so she was all about playing, 24/7. I flew over to Australia with Anelise and Kristin on this enormous two-decker plane. I sat downstairs with my family; on the upper level of the plane was all party. It was Leonardo DiCaprio (always Leo), Jonah Hill, Nas, the Fugees, nightclub owner Jason Strauss… The list went on and on—a slew of celebrities, all together upstairs for the twenty-hour flight. I was confronted with my two worlds, converging in the same space—Jamie Foxx the party guy and Jamie Foxx the family guy.

Maybe what I expected was like a sitcom episode where a guy has two dates on the same night and keeps jumping back and forth between the two. I don't know why I thought that would work, considering every one of those sitcom episodes ends with the guy getting busted and losing both dates. But when party Jamie and family Jamie met face-to-face, it was clear who was gonna win. Family Jamie every time.

I could hear the club music pounding upstairs, *boom boom boom*, while I was sitting next to Anelise watching *The Little Mermaid*. I kept trying to ignore the party music by singing along to the movie louder. But I found myself like mermaid Ariel, looking up, wishing I could be PART OF THAT WOOOOORLD.

My phone kept ringing with my guys calling me from upstairs.

"You comin' up?" my longtime friend and personal assistant Dave Brown asked. Dave's daughter is close in age to Anelise, but she had stayed home. Dave was rolling solo—and looking for his wingman.

"Maaaan, I'll get killed if I come up there!" I whispered to him into the phone.

Anelise was watching me closely. "Are you going up?" she asked.

"Nooo! Why would I want to go up there?" I said. Why would I wanna go eat crab legs with superstars when I can watch a crab sing about how cool living under the sea is, for the fifth time in a row? Why the hell do kids love watching the same movie over and over?

I kept hearing *pop pop pop* sounds. Champagne bottles. For twenty straight hours. Damn. But I never went upstairs. I stayed with my family through the entire flight. And I had a great time with them. When we finally landed in Australia, the parties split into two separate vacations—there was the family stuff for me and there was the frolic for my dudes. My family and I were gonna go see some koala bears at the zoo while the other dudes were going to something called a "champagne bar"—as if these motherfuckers needed more champagne. Soon after the zoo, we took a boat excursion with other families and kids, enjoying the lovely views of the Australian coastline. *Wow, this is beautiful. So much fun*, I was thinking. My phone rang. I looked down—it was DiCaprio.

"Yo, pal, can you break away?" he asked.

"What you got going on?"

"Well, there's a boat coming by. You'll see in a second."

Right on cue, a gorgeous boat came drifting by. The scene onboard looked crazy, like somebody had transported a Hollywood Hills mansion onto the water: multiple hot tubs, a pool, tons of food (is that actually Mr. Chow?). My eyes bulged. I spotted Leo, waving at me. I gotta admit, I was a little jealous. I had to keep reminding myself that the joy of spending time with my children trumped multiple hot tubs. But damn, my back muscles started relaxing just looking at those jets.

As they drove by, I could only shake my head. I felt something tugging at my shorts. I looked down; it was Anelise.

"Daddy, we play?" she said.

I nodded. "Okay, let's play, baby. Let's play."

Of course, had my daughter not been there with me, I would have been all over that boat. But this was Grown-Up Jamie. This was Sagittarius Man 2.0— the Sag who had been dedicated to being a kid, now grown up and just enjoying his kids. In the end, I didn't regret my decision for a minute. Seriously.

C'mon, why don't you believe me?

While we were in Australia, I was communicating with Corinne the whole time. She couldn't make the trip to Australia, but she was going to meet us in Las Vegas, where we would bring in the New Year together—the second time for me. Corinne was surely aware that I was in Australia having a wonderful time with Anelise. I would have to make up for that in Vegas with her.

I didn't find out until recently that she had a running joke with her friends: "Hey, did you see the latest thing that your father didn't invite you to?" It was painful for me to hear that. I told her, "Corinne, I never even thought you wanted to be invited." I would invite her to stuff and she'd never want to go. She was busy doing her own thing, her grown-woman thing. But after she told me about the joke, I would be sure to call her. Eventually it became our own little joke, because she'd always tell me, "Oh, Dad, I can't make that one. Thank you anyway!"

But what I realized was that she just wanted me to make the effort to invite her. In other words, at least invite me—so I can tell you "No."

So on this particular New Year's Eve, with 2012 flipping to 2013, I had come up with an elaborate plan for me to pick up Corinne and her friends when our party jet landed in Vegas. This, I wouldn't let her say no to. She was partying with me.

Corinne was eighteen at the time, about to turn nineteen six weeks later. I was excited to see her and get the New Year's Eve party started. We arrived in Vegas at 11:20 p.m., so there wasn't a lot of time to spare. We rushed to the club where I had planned for us to see the fireworks and do the countdown. I was crushed when the bouncers at the door peered at Corinne and her two friends and told me they couldn't come in. They had to be twenty-one. I looked at Corinne's face and saw the tears well up.

She had warned me that she wouldn't be let in, but I got too cocky. I guess when you're a movie star, enough people say yes to you that you stop planning on hearing a no.

"Dad, I knew it! I knew it! You ruined it. You ruined our New Year's!"

I felt horrible. But I couldn't give up that easily. I was determined to make this right. The clock was ticking. It was 11:45—New Year's Eve was going to happen without us. But what could I do? I had just fifteen minutes to figure something out.

"What am I going to tell my friends, Dad?" Corinne said. "You're embarrassing me!"

Fuck, fuck, fuck! I was panicking. This was supposed to be my special night with Corinne. And I was blowing it. I had fucked up again. An old Black female security guard had been watching us. She saw the panic on my face and extended a hand of mercy.

"You know, my husband is working security upstairs at this little party," she said in my ear. "I could try to get you guys in there because you don't need ID."

Yes! I was so grateful I could have kissed her on the lips. But we didn't have much time for all that—it was 11:53. We followed the woman onto the elevator. Because we had only minutes to spare, she first tried to get off at the hotel pool. But as soon as we got outside, we heard a stern male voice.

"What are you guys doing here?" he said, as he moved toward us. "You can't be here. This is where all of the fireworks are being set off. It's a fire hazard!"

11:55.

My head was about to explode.

"Dad, I knew it!" Corinne said, again in tears.

But the old lady hadn't given up yet. She had called her husband.

"Come on!" she said. We piled onto a private elevator. We went up up up. When the doors opened, we stepped out to the sounds of Abba's "Dancing Queen" blasting from the speakers, being sung by a live band. My heart sank. "Dancing Queen"? Where the fuck were we?

But we kept moving toward the big windows. As soon as we stepped in front, the sky lit up with a bang. The fireworks had begun. It was midnight.

In classic Corinne style, she looked at me with a big smile on her face.

"Thank you, Dad," she said. I leaned in and gave her a kiss. Finally, a dad win.

"Dad, I'm sorry," she said. "Thank you. I appreciate it."

"Corinne, *I'm* so sorry," I said. "I just…you know, I always want you to be happy. Sometimes, I…it just feels like I'm fucking up."

I knew that things sometimes weren't perfect during Corinne's childhood, so it hurt me when I disappointed her.

"No, Dad, it's good," she said.

"You know I love you?" I said.

"Dad, it's fine. You know, we made it."

I looked up with a smile and gestured toward the bandstand.

"Well, what about this band?"

"I actually like the band," she said with a laugh.

As if on cue, the band broke into the Wild Cherry 1970s classic, "Play That Funky Music (White Boy)."

"Yeah, they were dancing and singing...Come on, ladies and gentlemen!" the lead singer called out.

Corinne and I couldn't help but crack up. It was perfect. In a weird way, the band, the party, the atmosphere, were more her speed than the club where we were originally going. It was steak and potatoes, not Mr. Chow's. It turned out to be the perfect party for her and her friends. They appreciated the effort I had made.

In many ways, that entire trip was an accurate metaphor for fatherhood. Sometimes you have to choose *The Little Mermaid* with your baby girl over parties with your homies. And when you really put yourself out there on behalf of your kids, when you make every effort to create a flawless night, even if you fail miserably, in the end they will appreciate how much you tried. It's something fathers always need to remember: It's not really about how it turned out. They just want to know you care. Corinne saw all the effort and the angst right before her eyes.

After that, another friend of mine, a nightclub owner, invited us to a private party he was throwing.

"Richie, man, I'm in a tight situation," I told him. "Listen, my daughter and her friends are with me, and they won't let them in the club. And it's New Year's Eve."

"Are you fucking kidding me?" he said. "Shut up, bro. Where are they? Come on, let's go. Let's go! Shut up, I don't want to hear nothing. Let's go."

When we got to the party, Corinne was overjoyed when she looked around and saw Paula Patton and Robin Thicke, who at the time were married and were two of her favorite celebrities. She was used to celebrities, but in her mind some of them rose above.

I sat back with my drink and just smiled as I watched her and her friends have the time of their young lives. My job was complete. It didn't even matter if I enjoyed myself that night. It was all about Corinne.

GETTING ROASTED

Anelise is the world's foremost expert on Jamie Foxx's weaknesses. I thought the teenage years were for making your parent's life hell, but I guess Anelise got a head start. As a comic, I'm used to being roasted and even more used to dishing it right back out. But it's not really a fair fight with my daughter—because she seems to be able to say whatever the hell she wants and I'm supposed to be "an adult" or "mature" or whatever and not fire back!

We were sitting at the dinner table a couple years ago with many of my family members who live with me. The subject bounced around to zodiac signs. People were listing the attributes of their signs when

Anelise, without even looking up from the video game on her phone, felt the need to weigh in.

"My dad's a Sagittarius and they say Sagittariuses have trouble committing in their relationships," she said. I was like, *What?*

Everybody stopped talking for a second, marveling at this observation from a ten-year-old kid.

"Anelise, how do you know about relationships?" one of my cousins asked her.

She shrugged. "Relationships is when you really love somebody and you care about them. That's what relationships are."

"But what do you know about that?" somebody else asked.

"Well, that's what they say about Sagittarius. You can read it."

But I can't hit her back. I can't say, "Oh, we gonna talk about relationships, you little Libra? Let's see how well you do in a relationship if you're self-indulgent, controlling and vindictive!" Yeah, that's right. I know about the zodiac.

Moments like that keep me grounded, no matter how much success and accolades come my way outside the house. Kids get a thrill from messing with you. And I'm not alone in that. Dave Brown, one of my best friends, has a daughter who is close to Anelise's age. And one night, Dave's daughter called him out so hard in front of a lot of people.

"My dad is a liar," Dave's daughter declared.

The room exploded. "Oh shit!" we all shouted out at once.

"What do you mean I lie, Gabby?" Dave asked her.

"Sometimes when you're on the phone, you say you're on your way but you got to go pick up your daughter. And I'm sitting right next to you. You're lying."

We had to explain to her that's not actually lying, we're just trying to get off the phone. "Well, you shouldn't lie," she said. "You should just say 'I want to get off the phone.'"

Good luck raising your kids not to lie and then trying to explain to them that some lies are okay. A small "we're just trying not to hurt their feelings" will bite you in the ass when they lie about their grades. "I didn't lie about my F in math, I just didn't want to hurt your feelings that you did such a poor job parenting me that I failed basic arithmetic."

The thing about kids is I don't know if they don't understand nuance or that they perfectly understand nuance but choose to be literal whenever it's helpful to them.

Once, when I got mad because Anelise was spending too much time on her phone, I lashed out.

"Listen, can you get off your phone for two minutes?!" I said.

I watched her go to the clock app and set the timer to two minutes before she sat the phone down.

"Anelise, if you don't turn that goddamn timer off..."

"Well, you said two minutes," she said.

"I don't mean literally."

"Then you should say what you mean."

I shook my head. "Alright, Anelise, eighteen minutes."

I was midsentence when that buzzer went off and she was back on TikTok faster than I could say "Tik."

Anelise is never shy about clowning me, and that's not just limited to retorts to what I say. Just ask my hairline. Full disclosure: Over the years, as my hair has started to turn gray, I have employed a team of professionals to keep my shit right. Brother can't be going gray, right? One of the tools we employ is black hair dye. Anelise and her cousins are always in my room, running through all my stuff, and they opened a drawer and saw the little container of black dye for my hair. She held it up one day.

"Dad, like what's really going on with your hair?" she said, laughing. "Forget all of the fame and stuff, what is going on with those grays?" She's behind the curtain, watching the wizard pulling levers to make the transformation to a perfect head of hair and beard, and she enjoys the hell out of it. Those are the real daddy-daughter moments, where you're completely unmasked.

One time, when we were going somewhere on a very windy day, I looked over at Anelise, who was cracking up.

"What's up?" I asked her.

"Dad! You gotta go back," she said.

"What?"

"The wind blew all the black dye out your hair!"

"Oh, man. How's it look?"

"Dad, it ain't good!" she said. "You have to go back—'cause you don't want people to catch you out here like this." We shared a laugh.

Kids push boundaries. That's normal, it's healthy and it should piss you the hell off. But as long as they aren't crossing some wild line, the thing you gotta do as a parent is take a few Ls here and there. Let them find their voice. For now. Once Anelise is grown, she better get ready to go toe-to-toe with me. And watch out, Anelise. I'm a Sagittarius. We can go hard.

GUNS VS. GUCCI

As I've said, one way that I try to keep my head on straight in Hollywood is by carrying as much of Texas around with me as I can. LA is the world capital of passive-aggressiveness—everyone smiling in your face, making brunch plans for the weekend and then, whether it's talking shit behind your back or stabbing you in the back, it's *something* going on behind your back. Texas is the world capital of saying what the fuck you mean. I still get shocked faces at a party in the Hollywood Hills when I say, "I thought that movie was bullshit." Everyone knows someone who knows someone who was an associate producer on that movie (whatever the fuck "associate producer" means), so it's better for your career to be polite. But I find it's a lot easier to live life by just being honest and saying what's on your mind. And that all comes from Texas.

The best place to start painting Texas is at our family reunions, which are wild. It's a collection of people I've borrowed from liberally over the years in creating characters for my comedy. My mother's biological family, the Rosebuds, were like hood superheroes. #GhettoAvengers. All of them were good-looking, but they were not to be played with. There was an element of danger to them. Because the neighborhood they lived in was much more hood than it was Pleasantville, everybody needed their own special power to protect themselves. My mother's special skill was being good with her hands, so she didn't need any weapons. She could fight. One aunt was an expert with a knife, while another was good with guns. Then there was Aunt V, who was skilled with both knives and guns.

When I was six, I walked up to the house in South Dallas and I saw my uncle sitting on the porch, wielding a knife next to a pile of bullets. Slowly, carefully, he was putting an X on the tip of each bullet.

"Unc, what you doin' with bullets and a knife?" I asked.

"Hey, look here," he said, holding up one of the bullets so I could see it. "When the bullet hit the skin, it split."

I wasn't old enough yet to be cursing, but if I did curse I would have said, "What the fuck?!"

Yeah, my family is filled with more than its share of crazy. And I love every single one of their eccentric asses. It's better to be real and flawed than phony. When you're phony, you're not truly connecting with people, and what's the point of life if you're not connecting with other people?

I try to make sure my daughter Anelise is influenced by my folks in Texas as much as she's influenced by whoever the fuck's on TikTok. Keep her stamped with the DNA of South Dallas and Terrell.

When I tell her my Dallas family members are coming to visit us in California, Anelise gets excited. I was giddy when I saw that she had picked up certain things over the years. Made me see that Dallas was seeping in. For instance, she has developed a deep love for Lawry's seasoning salt. I know that's pure South Dallas. If you don't know Lawry's...that probably means you're white. Black people put Lawry's on everything—BBQ, burgers, steak...We ain't even need salt and pepper! You truly ain't Black if you ain't got Lawry's in your cabinet.

You know how else I knew Texas was in Anelise's blood? When I found out how much she likes guns. When you grow up in Texas, guns are like opinions—everybody has one. In some quarters, they practically give kiddies a rifle instead of a pacifier. The people who inhabit my world in LA would sooner give their kids a line of cocaine than a gun. Two very different places. But Anelise is way more Texas than LA when it comes to this stuff. I first noticed when she was playing video games: If it had a gun, she couldn't wait to use it to take out everything on the screen—zombies, cartoon elks, bad guys, it didn't matter. One time, she was shooting Tetris pieces and I was like, "When in the hell did you get a gun in Tetris?!" I gave her more than a few worried looks. What does this mean? Should we be alarmed? Do we need guns to protect ourselves from her?!

But she hadn't yet asked for a gun...Instead she asked for a *bow and arrow*. A bit concerning, but I wasn't about to mess with a girl who wants a bow and arrow. I obliged and took her down to the local Big 5 Sporting Goods store. We passed by a gun display—or I should say that *I* passed by the gun display. Anelise froze, staring at the selection.

"Do you want to try some guns instead?" I asked her. But it wasn't a real question. I already knew the answer.

"Yeah, that's what I want to do!" she said excitedly. I admit that, as a father, I probably should've thought this through. But, as a Texan...yee-haw, you're gonna try some guns—responsibly.

So we picked up a couple of air rifles and brought

them home. We went out in the backyard for target practice with our new purchases.

"Listen. You got to be very serious when it comes to safety," I told her before we started. "Anytime you giggle or laugh, we're going to stop."

She giggled right away, so I made her put down the weapon and we took a break. She looked at me. *Oh, Dad is serious.*

"This is not a laughing matter," I said.

But once we got past that boring shit, it was time for the fun stuff. And she impressed me right away with her focus.

"Okay, let's see what you can do." I set up a few cans on the fence and then realized I should've probably set them up a lot closer or at least used bigger cans, but—the girl proceeded to blow away all of them on her first try!

"Whoa!" My mind started racing. Oh my God, my child is a natural! The next Annie Oakley even. I was already planning for the biathlon in the Winter Olympics.

"Anelise, how are you this good at shooting a gun?" I asked.

"Dad! Because I play video games."

Of course. I shook my head. Those damn video games.

I told her to do it again. And she did. And I filmed it.

I walked away that day very proud of my daughter. But I hesitated about sharing this video on my social media platforms. Don't get me wrong, I was just as guilty as the other parents in my circle of participating in that unspoken kid competition. You know the one I'm talking about.

Look at what my daughter can do! She can play football! There's a touchdown!

But look at what my daughter can do! She can play basketball! There's a three-pointer!

It's just social media here is different than it is in Texas. My Texas homies aren't spending hours every day on social media looking for clicks. In my everyday LA world, it feels like everybody wants to get noticed, everybody is desperate for those shares and likes. The latest gossip scandal is always at the tip of everyone's tongue. You can only post sanctioned things. You gotta worry about the 1 percent of people who may be offended by something (or usually anything).

So I nixed the social media idea and just sent it to a few California friends. A little nervous about the blowback but I had to brag about my daughter. Still, I got none of the usual exclamations of how awesome it was. Instead, I got silence. They were probably thinking, *Damn, when did Jamie join the NRA?* And who wants to be seen applauding a kid with a gun? But c'mon, it's my daughter with a gun! And she's hitting bull's-eye after bull's-eye!

Sometimes the Texas in Anelise shocks LA folk. But the reverse is also true. Anelise has Hollywood pumping in her blood. One time, I had one of my best friends from Texas over to my house with his wife. Remember, these are nice Texans who aren't quite used to Hollywood craziness. We got to talking about how much Anelise likes to write stories and how good she is. They asked her to tell them what her last story was about, so Anelise went into the pitch.

"It starts at a school. The principal is Satan and he's trying to steal the students' souls," Anelise began. That's when I realized there might be a bit of a culture clash—my friends shifted uncomfortably in their seats. Oh, I should probably mention they're pretty hard-core Christians, especially the wife. I knew they wouldn't be expecting my cute little girl to be talking about Satan, let alone talking about the students all going to hell, which was structured like a video game where the only way they could move up in the levels was to give themselves over to Satan! All the while, the principal is trying to get them to worship the Devil. (It's really clever, right? My baby is talented!) I glanced over at my friend's wife, and she looked like she was about a half second from calling a priest.

"What's wrong, Dad?" Anelise asked when she saw the somewhat concerned expression on their faces. *Oh, you can't tell what's wrong, Anelise? That you're telling a couple Baptists a story about children worshipping the Devil? They're looking at you like you're Rosemary's Baby!* But even those devout Christians could recognize some good storytelling—they wouldn't let her stop until they found out what happened. I guess the Devil won in the end!

So my daughters aren't full Texan and they aren't full Californian, and I like it that way. The truth is that being too much of one thing is never good. The best part of raising my daughters with perspectives from both worlds is they can make choices for themselves. "I like this part of being a Texan, I like this part of being a California girl, etc., etc." And as a parent, yes, it's your job to instill the values you grew up with (Texan for me), but you also gotta push them to explore other things and make them their own. Just be careful if they go too far, because they might need an exorcism.

THE KING'S GAMBIT

I lucked out with Corinne in the sense that she has no interest in staying mad. She can let things go. Anelise? Not so much.

One day when she was about five or six, she made an announcement.

"I'm mad," she said.

"What you mad about?" I asked.

"I'm mad about what happened yesterday," she said.

"But that was yesterday."

"Well, I'm gonna be mad the rest of the day."

"Anelise, that was yesterday, you said it was—"

"I'll be mad until I don't want to be mad anymore," she interrupted.

I chuckled to myself. "Alright," I said. "Well, I'll be here when you get unmad."

When she'd get angry, she'd tell us it was right there in her head while she pointed to her noggin. One time when my sister Deidra—who is very much like Anelise—was with us, she said, "I have that same thing! Anger that just simmers."

Damn, suddenly we were in *The Shining*.

I needed to teach Anelise about forgiveness and letting go, which was tough because I myself have held on to bitterness about my mother's absences for a long time. As I began to understand some of the hardships my mother overcame in her life, forgiving her became easier.

My mom's seventy-eight now and we're living in the same house (we'll get to that story), but I'm still trying to recover from all those years when she wasn't around. I have talked to my daughters about my early relationship with my mother, or lack of one, to give them a sense of why I believe it's important to forgive and try to re-engage. Sometimes though, it's easier to say than do. With my biological father, I didn't do a very good job of reconnecting. I had to do a lot of work to get to a point where I could let go of the anger I had. I made some strides in forgiving my father, but I never got all the way there.

My father found his place in the Muslim community in South Dallas, where he had a whole different family after he split with my mom. I got an opportunity to meet them and hang out a few times, which I thought was fun. At least I got a chance to see my dad. He was married to a Muslim woman who wasn't quite as observant as him—which was always so surprising to me. I can see getting over certain differences in marriage—"I like action movies, you like romantic comedies, let's take turns picking movies"—but my dad was strict in his religion. I guess love overshadows things, and they had several children together. The few times I was around his wife I thought she was a lot funnier than my father, with a bit of hood in her. She was a beautiful woman with an engaging smile. She was also a security guard who carried a .357 Magnum, so I thought she was kinda cool (and I knew not to mess with her). She took pleasure in poking fun at him, which was something I had rarely seen, because he was so serious all the time. Or maybe he was also scared of her .357.

"Oh, he trying to get to heaven all the damn time, but I drink every once in a while!" she told me.

"Don't talk like that," he said, trying to shush her.

"Ah, Shahid, live your life and let me live mine!" she said, loudly. "So damn uptight."

I thought it was funny to see him uncomfortable; it made him seem warmer, more human. Seeing him human gave me hope that we'd have a close father-son relationship. What also gave me hope was he would sometimes teach me things, things that I still hold to this day. I guess I've always been like a cactus, I never needed much water to grow. [Note for readers: The "water" in the last sentence was a metaphor. When it comes to literal water, I drink a lot of it. It is very important to stay hydrated, especially if you're an athlete.] One thing he taught me was about the power of visualization—long before I ever heard anybody else talking about it. He instructed me on envisioning what my future would look like, what success would look like. When I was a high jumper in high school, we talked about it during one of his visits. He asked me what was going on in my world.

"I'm a senior and I think I might be able to go to state."

That's the Texas Relays, which was a huge deal in a state as big as Texas. At the time I was ranked fourth in my district and twenty-second in the state. "Fantastic," he said, as he often would.

"Son, I want to know—what is your approach?"

Approach? Damn, is it that serious? I just run as fast as I can and jump as high as I can.

"Let me give you some advice," he said. "Come sit." We were at my place and he asked me to lay back on the bed with him. "Find a spot on the wall, look at that spot and envision yourself not just jumping but running, jumping—" Then he had to ask, "You clear the bar, right?" I thought this was crazy as hell, but I'm already laying in bed with him, might as well imagine myself jumping.

"Yeah, Dad, I clear the bar."

"Envision yourself being light as a feather but strong as a horse. Lifting over that bar, landing and receiving the awards you were to be given."

"Dad, I love that. It's not awards though. They give you medals."

"Whatever it is, keep in mind, when you see it, you can be it," he said.

I've always held on to this. Whether it works or not, I visualize still. I visualized winning the Best Actor Oscar for *Ray*. But to be fair, I also visualized winning an Oscar for *Booty Call* and ended up losing to Jack Nicholson. (I mean, I wasn't nominated either, but technically every actor who acted in 1997 lost to Jack Nicholson.)

I guess he liked teaching me ways to use my mind. When I was eight, he also taught me an incredible game: chess. Everybody in my neighborhood was playing checkers, but he wanted me to learn chess. There's a reason the idiom goes "This is chess, not checkers." Chess challenges you to think ahead, think on different levels, think what your opponent is thinking. As he broke down all the pieces, each of their special powers on the board, I started imagining them coming alive, like real-life characters. I was like that girl from *Queen's Gambit* except I wasn't addicted to prescription pills.

Learning chess isn't just about learning chess. One time we were playing early on and I used my queen too soon. He took my queen and watched my game fall apart.

"You have to learn to play without your queen," he said. "You have to learn to play without certain pieces." Do I have to? Can't I just resign and start a new game?

One game it came down to just his king and a pawn, and I watched him demolish me with that one pawn.

"Sometimes it'll get down to just you and nearly nothing. Which means you're really trusting in yourself. As long as you're trusting in yourself, it doesn't matter what kingdom is against you."

Damn, that's deep. I thought we were just playing a game. I didn't know there was a whole damn kingdom against me!

Now, all these years later, wouldn't you know—what's Anelise's favorite game? Chess. I taught it to her and explained that there's a man she never met, a man I barely knew, who gave me great things I want to pass on to her. I tried teaching her the other lessons, but every time I try to take her queen, or even her pawns, she whups my ass. I guess *she* is more like the girl from *Queen's Gambit* than I was. I'll just make sure she stays away from prescription pills and booze.

My father and I hadn't kept in touch after I moved to Hollywood. But one day, out of nowhere, he reached out to say that he was coming to Los Angeles. I was so excited. I was already starring in *The Jamie Foxx Show* and I couldn't wait to show him my world. However, when he got here, he couldn't care less about show business. Damn, not even a "Hey, you got a show named after you on TV?! That's fantastic!" No matter what age you are, you still want some sort of approval from your parents.

When he showed up, the first thing I noticed was he had many teeth missing. I was shocked.

"Whoa, Pop, how you doin'?"

"Oh, I'm fantastic!" he said.

"Are you sure you're fantastic?" I said, pointing to his mouth. "'Cause your grill is messed up."

"Well, you know, the Honorable Elijah Muhammad said he would provide..."

"He's gonna provide you with a root canal and some dentures?" I made a joke of it because I could tell he was a little embarrassed. I was embarrassed too. I didn't really want people to know me and my father hadn't been connected over the years. I had painted a somewhat embellished picture of him to my friends in Hollywood as this great guy who was always around, proud of me, had a full white smile. But *shit*, we were in Hollywood—everybody's lying.

"Pops, regardless of that, I got everything planned. We can go see Hollywood. We can maybe go to Disneyland, see some other places. And maybe you even can get your dental work done."

But it turned out my dad didn't want his son's opinion on things. Only the Honorable Elijah Muhammad's.

"The Honorable Elijah Muhammad appreciates all those things. But I was wondering if you could come to the mosque with me."

"Mosque?" I knew what a mosque was, I was just caught off guard.

"The mosque. That's where we fellowship. I would love to have you there and show you my religion."

I was now a grown man in my thirties—I had made up my mind about my own faith. I didn't need him to try to convert me.

"Pops, we can do all that, but I wanted to do some things where it was just me and you, just enjoying each other's company."

He pushed back. "I would love for you to come…" and he went on about the Honorable Elijah Muhammad.

"Pops, I can't do it. First of all, you don't have any teeth in your mouth. What are people gonna say about me—*I can't provide for my dad's teeth*? How about we go to the dentist and we do these other things?"

We went on jousting back and forth—until I realized he needed to go to the mosque first because Minister Farrakhan was speaking. And then it slowly and painfully dawned on me: That's why he came to LA. It wasn't to stay with me. He just needed a place to crash. I got upset, a bit hurt. I felt this was the opportunity for me to pick up on a lot of lost time. My anger boiled up, but not to the point of cursing him out or telling him to get out of my house.

I decided to big-shot him. To make him feel as small as he made me feel. I simply told him that I actually knew Minister Farrakhan. His jaw dropped. It's like if he would have told me that he knew Prince.

"You know the Minister Farrakhan?"

"Yes, I do," I said. "As a matter of fact, he was the one who presided over Rick James's funeral when he passed away." *Boom*.

"Why Rick James?"

"Because Rick James was one of his friends."

"Really? But the Honorable Elijah Muhammad—"

"Yeah. Still doesn't mean he couldn't be friends with the man," I said, interrupting him. "I actually paid for Rick James's funeral, and the reception after the service was here at the house, where Minister

Farrakhan sat right over there." I pointed to a spot in the living room where Farrakhan and others sat and fellowshipped and told stories about Rick James. Maybe it wasn't nice lording this over my father, but he was so close-minded that I felt he needed a bit of a shock to his system.

He shook his head; he couldn't understand it.

"Dad, listen. Your son has done well for himself. Part of becoming successful in this business is I get a chance to meet a lot of interesting people. Had you stayed connected to me, you'd be meeting these people as well. But I'm going to tell you this: I love you—but I'm not going to the mosque. I will, however, get you a hotel. I will make sure you're set up for whatever you need to do at the mosque. And I want you to have a fantastic time." Let it be known that I didn't care what religion he was; he could have been Jewish, Baptist, Rastafari, or Seventh Day Adventist for all I cared, I just wanted and needed his time.

That was the last time my father and I spoke. I wished we could have made a connection. I didn't wish him any ill will though. Over the years, my stepfather, who I called Pops, would sometimes tell me my biological father had contacted him to try to reach me. I appreciate Pops for being a grown man and not locking my father out or telling him not to call. He would entertain him and have conversations with him. More than once, he said to me, "Your father called—you think you want to talk to him?"

"Pops, I just can't do it," I explained. I'm not sure whether I was right or wrong. I tell my daughters that sometimes your parents can be wrong— it shouldn't always be my way or the highway, as if there's only one way. Except me. This parent cannot be wrong.

One day Pops told me, "Your father passed away."

It came as a shock but I didn't feel what I thought I would feel, which is disappointment and despair. I ended up not feeling anything. The relationship was dead for so long, I had already mourned it many times over. But I did send him a spiritual blessing: I told him I hoped what he was looking for in the spiritual world, he'd find. Although there weren't ill feelings, I chose not to go to his funeral. I don't know where that leaves me on the moral or spiritual scale.

It's tough to teach my daughters this lesson of forgiveness when there was never a beautiful, emotive reconciliation between me and my dad like at the end of a happy movie. The lesson I have for my daughters is that sometimes you just have to let go of things, of people, of emotions that are weighing you down.

I can't always control if I make my daughters mad

or not. I'm gonna mess up, embarrass them, God knows what. But I can control that I'll always be there for them when they get unmad. And on top of chess and visualization, that's the most important thing my father taught me—even though he taught it by not doing it. So if he is reading this book from the great beyond, my father should know he is still part of the reason I always do my best to be there for my kids.

LOVE & BASKETBALL & KNOWING WHEN TO KEEP YOUR MOUTH SHUT

It was important for me to raise my girls with a healthy sense of competitive spirit. And that's a light way of saying I wanted my girls to love sports as much as I did. In high school, I was all about football and still, to this day, rarely miss a Cowboys game. Or a Lakers game. Hey, I'm always going to root for LeBron James, but don't get it twisted: Cowboys for life. Roger Staubach was my hero growing up.

For Corinne, sports wasn't her bag—despite my efforts. She was tall, so we thought maybe running track would be her thing. But in the middle of the race, she would stop, wave to us and say, "Hi, guys!" Okay, maybe not track. She gave softball a try—until one day she lost a fly ball in the sun and it smashed into her face. *Kapow!* There was blood, stitches and a very angry black eye. After that, Corinne decided to leave the softball behind. She wound up using her organizing skills to create the cheerleading program at her high school, which is still thriving years after she graduated. It was a lovely compromise and confluence of her talents and interests.

Anelise was always more athletically inclined (not to mention tall as hell), and I never missed an opportunity to nurture that. When Anelise first started playing basketball, she was so tall that she played with the boys, one of only about three girls in the entire league. Remember that scene in *Air Bud* with the guy arguing with the ref, "There ain't no rule says a dog can't play basketball!"? Well, I was ready to be that guy at her school if they didn't let her play with the boys, but fortunately they did. Sure, they were wary, but they couldn't deny her hitting them three-pointers.

I went to support her at her first game, yelling out her point total every time she scored a basket. "Anelise, that's how we do, baby! In they face!"

And then I got hit with one of the craziest fucking things I've ever heard.

"Um, Mr. Foxx? We don't count the scores here," the woman who runs the team said to me. I'm sorry…You don't count *points*?! What the hell are we playing a GAME for? Let's stop counting points in Scrabble while we're at it. "Yes, honey, I see you played EMBEZZLEMENT and landed on triple letter and triple word squares, but I put down DOG so our scores are tied."

She went on to explain that they "didn't want anyone to think that they're failures because they didn't participate or score."

I shook my head. First of all, nobody's fooling anybody. If you're playing a game of basketball and you never get a shot in, you *know* that! You don't suddenly feel better because the teacher says the score was actually 0–0. But more importantly, not keeping score hides everyone's accomplishments. And kids need to be proud of what they accomplish. Especially my Anelise, who was not only playing with all boys but was housing it, killing 'em! I wanted her self-confidence built up. Not only is she playing with the boys, but she kickin' they ass.

While I thought competition was healthy and pushed you to be the best version of yourself, this school was the exact opposite. Not keeping score was the tip of the iceberg. They were so serious about discouraging competition that they would play—wait for it—soccer with no ball. I'm just going to take a pause here so you could visualize that . . . . Got the picture?

They would run up and down the field, pretending they were kicking the ball, and wait for the teacher to yell out instructions.

"Okay, Billy, you have the ball now. Take a shot!" the teacher would say. And then Billy would pretend he was shooting at the goal. The first time I saw it, my head nearly combusted. #WhatTheEntireFuck-IsThis? I started messing with them. Whenever they would mime kicking the ball, I would mime getting hit in the face with the ball. I'd fall to the ground screaming. "Ahhh!! You got me right in the teeth!" Eventually they politely asked me to stop coming by "soccer" practice.

But back to American sports. I love watching Anelise play basketball. But I'm not planning on coddling her either. She didn't seem to mind not keeping score, but I want to raise tough, successful kids, and competition helps with that. I want them to know that they will have some successes and also some failures, and there's oftentimes reasons behind the successes and failures. For instance, if you don't put in the time to practice, you very well may suck—and I'm not going to come along and say that you were great when you weren't. I tell Anelise all the time, "Hey, if you want people to watch you and marvel at what you do, you got to put the work in." This reminds me of a great quote the philosopher Jay-Z said: "People only emulate the end result, not the process." That's some real shit right there.

I told her that maybe the school feels a certain way about competition and that everyone is equal, all that kumbaya, blah blah blah, but that's not how it's going down in the Foxx household. Shit, I'm in an industry that judges people every second of every day. If you don't have skin as thick as a rhino's hide, you ain't gonna make it. I know as my girls get more out into the real world, nobody's going to be taking it easy on them, talking about "Oh, don't worry, we're not going to keep score." Not only are they going to keep score, but as a woman and a woman of color, you're already 20 points down in the fourth quarter.

But I'm not just Anelise's coach. I'm also her dad. And knowing when to push, when to back off, when to let her quit, when to make her push outside her comfort zone—there's no parenting book on how to navigate this, not even this one. You gotta just be present and go with your gut.

My tough approach with Anelise hasn't been warmly received in all quarters of my family. My sister gets on me sometimes, telling me to ease off.

"You're talking to her like a son—you know she's a girl, right?" Deidra said to me one day.

"It shouldn't matter," I said. "She should still go hard and bust they ass."

But I worry sometimes that perhaps Deidra is right—maybe I am messing this up. I recently brought her to a Lakers game, thinking she might be inspired by watching one of her favorite players, LeBron James, the GOAT, do his thing. It looked like it was working for a while; Anelise was into the game, following closely. But by the third quarter, I look over at her after LeBron did a wild dunk and...she was back on her phone! At first I thought, *Oh, maybe she got that dunk on her Snapchat?* Nope! She's just texting with friends.

I raised Anelise to be strong, so I can't be too mad when she is being strongheaded. Nobody's going to force her to do anything or like anything until *she* decides. I got excited, probably too excited, when Anelise asked for the stretch pants with the pads on the knees that all the NBA players are wearing now under their uniforms. I asked her why she wanted them.

"Because I feel like being aggressive this year," she said.

Aww shit! I yelled inside. But then I told myself, *Don't fuck this up, Dad. Be chill.* I didn't say anything in response. I just nodded.

It was time for her first game of the new season. And I was keeping my mouth shut. As desperately as I wanted to keep giving her tips, I was too worried about driving her away from basketball. I already said plenty last season...enough that the school changed their policy and they were finally going to keep score! Hell yeah, finally the whole school can see my daughter win.

Or lose, I realized. Goddamn, I was an anxious mess. As her team was warming up, she missed a few free throws because she wasn't properly following through. I couldn't keep quiet any longer, and I yelled out, "Hand in the cookie jar!" miming the motion of putting your hand down in the cookie jar to simulate the proper follow-through. Anelise rolled her eyes so hard, and Deidra's voice was in my head, telling me to lay off.

And lay off I did. Even though Anelise towered over all the boys, looking like Yao Ming with big hair, her team couldn't hit a thing. They started down 9–0. And at this level, a nine-point deficit might as well be a thirty-point deficit, because kids can't really shoot yet. Or dribble. Honestly, children aren't that great at basketball. Not to brag, but I can crush any kid in a one-on-one pickup game.

I just had to watch my daughter get crushed and outplayed by players who I knew in my heart weren't better than her. And then it happened...During a time-out, Anelise came by and asked for advice. Well, would you look at that? When you're trying to help your kids, they know better, but when you stand back for a minute, suddenly it's "Daddy, can you help me?" Yes, I can. I told her to take charge, I told her to start trapping the other team in the backcourt. This time, there was no eye-rolling. She listened and fucking ran with it.

Under her leadership, they went out on the court a transformed team. They battled, grabbed rebounds, made steals. And Anelise kept scoring, soaking in the screams of the crowd. She got fouled and hit both free throws. As an aside, I have to tell you hitting both free throws in this league is so rare, it's about the equivalent of hitting a half-court shot.

We got to fifteen seconds left and we were down by three. Anelise turned to me again (I was practically the assistant coach by this point). This kid Tommy was a spunky little redhead who was having a memorable game. I told Anelise to get the ball to him. Would he hit a three-pointer? Doesn't matter, because I knew the other team would foul him. *Boom*, three free throws.

The first free throw, he made. Which came as a total shock to me because, like I said, these kids could barely hit the urinal, let alone hit free throws. But I didn't need lightning to strike two more times. What I needed was Anelise to get the rebound and immediately make a shot. I looked over at her...She was ready.

What happened next was in slow motion, like a scene from a Disney film. Tommy's free throw went up and fell short, bouncing off the front of the rim. Anelise blocked out the kid who was guarding her and caught the rebound. And she took her shot. And followed through. It looked exactly like she was putting her hand in the cookie jar. Looks like she listened to me after all. The ball fell through the hoop. Game tied, 23–23. The gym erupted into pandemonium.

The game went into two-minute overtime and Anelise's team lost, but it was still a wonderful— *psych!* What kind of bummer-ass ending to the story would that be? Anelise dominated overtime and they won 27–23.

That game changed everything. It had an enormous impact on her self-esteem, her feelings about basketball and, I think, perhaps her faith in her dad's approach to sport. She loved the acclaim she got from the crowd, which I think was perhaps even more extreme because Anelise was one of only two girls on the floor. Her friends ran from the stands to mob her. Her teammates would have carried her on their shoulders if they weren't little pip-squeaks. Even players and parents from the other team were congratulating her.

I watched her beaming face and knew she enjoyed it all.

"How do you feel about basketball now?" I asked.

"Dad, I love it!" she said.

I had about fifteen other things to say, but I let

it go. If I had hit her with the "I told you so," we would have taken nine steps backward. For once, I didn't get in my own way. It was one of the most exhilarating days I have had with Anelise since she was born. And it wouldn't have had the same impact if they played without an actual basketball, just miming the shots going in.

THAT GOOD OLD FAMILY DRAMA

If you pick a random married couple with a child and get to know them, you'll find there's drama and complications there. Now pick a random divorced couple with a child and get to know *them*. There's ten times the drama and complication. Now take my family situation…that's a hell of a tangled web to navigate! And no one gives you a map on how to navigate it, you just gotta be like the sailors centuries ago, trying to follow the stars. The stars in this case are the girls. What's best for them?

No matter what, I've never taken the importance of cultivating a good bond between a child and their mom for granted. I unfortunately learned that the hard way since, like my father, my mother wasn't a huge part of my life growing up. Even after my mother moved out to California to live with me, it took a long time for us to get on the same page. I don't know how to step to her, open that emotional door and say, "Hey, maybe we should talk." Even if I confront her, for me it might turn out to be a sentence with no ending, no punctuation. Just an ongoing question: What if? What if she dropped me off at school? What if she had been around more? How would my life have changed?

When I was growing up, I wasn't even sure that my mother loved me. Certainly not in the way I wanted. I wanted what the other kids had: someone picking them up from school, showing up to their games, being, you know...a mom.

I didn't see her that often, maybe a few times a year. I sometimes could overhear my grandmother talking to her on the phone. "You come down here and see this boy! You tell this boy all the time that you coming and then you don't come."

She would tell me she would see me on Christmas, and then she wouldn't show up. I'd be sitting there all day, a little boy waiting to see his mommy, looking for confirmation of her love. *Is she coming? Is she coming?* I was disappointed because everybody else seemed like they had moms and dads. Yes, I had my grandparents, who I'm forever grateful for, but that's different. For one, they were old! Kids would be laughing about the old people there, and I'd know who they were talking about without even having to look. But I told myself that I didn't really care about that. I was wise enough to appreciate the home they provided for me, the love they showed me. Their age was not something to get all worked up about.

While they were being old, my mom was being young. She was twenty-five when she had me and she didn't want to slow down, 'cause she was young and fly, hanging out with all the young socialites in Dallas. She was really beautiful; she kind of resembled a young Whitney Houston—of course, before Whitney was *Whitney*.

She already wasn't living in Terrell by the time I could form memories, so when she would visit, it was a big event. She would ride into town driving the latest whip, looking like she just flew in from LA or New York City. And I guess to Terrell, Dallas was as big as those. It was usually Sunday when she would make her appearance. Where is everybody on Sunday in Terrell, including me? Church. There I was at the piano stool, being the soundtrack for people's prayers to hopefully be answered by God, but the secret prayer I was saying to myself was, *I hope my mother walks through those doors*. And when my prayers were occasionally answered, it felt like I was already in heaven. When she walked in, it seemed like the doors swung open without ushers even touching them. She floated in as if in slow motion, wearing the latest hairstyle, rocking the hottest clothes, letting it be known that she was in the house—of the Lord, that is. People would actually clap when she entered the room. Sometimes the preacher would try to get everyone's attention to remind them who they were there to worship, but usually he would just clap along.

There was nothing more satisfying to a kid who was missing his mom.

Guys who went to school with her would knock on my grandparents' door to see if Louise was in town. They were just taking a shot in the dark.

"Is Louise still here?" they'd ask when I answered the door.

"No, sir. Who are you?" Fucking showing up at my door, asking about my mama.

"Oh, we went to high school together. She was so beautiful. I just wanted to come by."

It was a little weird, but I guess I was happy that my mother was the talk of the town.

Just as soon as she appeared, she disappeared. Which, needless to say, crushed me every time. Although I'm sure she was happy to see me, I had the feeling that something else was calling her. But even the brief good memories I have of her have lasted a lifetime. Like the one time when she showed me where my athleticism comes from. I was telling her how good I was going to be in sports—that whenever I got on the football field or the track, I was going to be the fastest man in the land. Can you blame me for showboating? I wanted to impress her. As ridiculous as it sounds, maybe subconsciously I thought I could impress her enough to get her to stay.

She looked at me and, in her Rosebud family manner, said, "You ain't fast."

"Ma, what you mean?"

"You ain't fast," she repeated. "I'm trying to tell you, you ain't fast. You think you can really run?"

"Yeah, I can run!"

"Well, I bet you a dollar to a donut you can't outrun me," she said.

"C'mon, Ma, don't make me burn your brakes off."

She looked at me. "Please! You ain't gonna never burn my brakes off. You have to understand where I'm from. I'm from sunny South Dallas. You gotta be able to run—from everything."

"What does being from South Dallas have to do with anything about your legs moving fast?"

"You'll see," she said, nodding confidently. She looked up ahead. "Race you to the dumpster. Bet you can't keep up."

"I don't have no money to bet. But I'm gonna outrun you."

"Anytime you ready, you take off," she said, smiling at me.

"Huh?"

"Dumpster. Make it easy on yourself—take off when you're ready."

In my mind I was thinking, *I hate to have to burn my mom like this, but it's about to be on.* I took off. I just knew I was killing her. As I started to look back, thinking it was over, I saw that not only was she gaining on me, but she was laughing at the same time as she started to pass me.

"Boy, I told you that you ain't fast," she said as she got to the dumpster. At least I think that's what she said. I was too busy holding my side and catching my breath.

She was somewhat playing the part of attentive parent, but I always had the feeling that in the back of her head she was listening to some kind of part-time-mom alarm clock, waiting for it to go off and let her know it was time to get back to her other life—one that didn't include me. We would laugh and have a great time, but then I could sense her getting antsy. Checking her watch, replying to me with shorter and shorter sentences. Time to split.

With my kids, I'd start to worry while I was gone for a while, shooting a movie. I didn't wanna just pop into my daughters' lives between jobs and leave them with a few memories of me beating them in a footrace. I wanted them to have shitloads of memories of me beating them in footraces, tennis, basketball, chess, etc., etc. Okay, they're allowed to win a few too. Of course, there were times when I couldn't make it to something important. But there were also times when I would take a red-eye across the country just to attend a school meeting.

Still, I saw when Corinne moved into her adolescent years that there were things she just wasn't comfortable sharing with me. There was a whole separate category of "mom issues." She needed the counsel of someone who could identify with what her body was going through, how her mind was developing, how she will be seen by the world. Puberty hits everyone like a sack of bricks. Not only does your body change but also who you're comfortable talking to about it (read: not Dad). Although I understood all that, it wasn't easy to accept.

But I learned how much I was out of the loop when Corinne was sixteen. We were on our way to dinner when I found out that my daughter was dealing with anxiety. She had been struggling for a whole year and nobody told me. I was devastated; I fell apart, reacting impulsively, going from zero to one hundred. I was so angry. I was angry that Corinne kept it from me and felt that she couldn't talk to me about it.

I was still boiling mad but I knew how to deal with it. Here's my advice for anyone when you're seeing red: Ask yourself why you're angry and make yourself spell it out. You'll notice that usually it's several things mixed together you're mad about. Good, now separate them. And second, try to get more specific about what you're feeling than the word "mad."

I was mad Corinne didn't confide in me—then I realized, I was *hurt*. I was bitter that Corinne and I didn't have the kind of relationship where we could talk about things like that. I was worried about Corinne and about the things in her life causing her anxiety. I felt powerless in the situation and vulnerable—maybe I was doing something wrong as a father that created the environment where secrets were kept from me. But I'm glad I processed some of these emotions first, and then I called up my sister and some of my friends to share my devastation.

"Man, family gonna be family, family gonna have all kinds of shit," one of my old heads told me. "Shit you didn't never know. And when you find out, you gonna be flabbergasted and shit like that. You just got to know how to pivot."

So I pivoted and had an honest talk with Corinne. I decided to go easy, out of fear that I could do more damage if I pressed her too hard. But I'm her dad! What was happening to my baby?

But as boxed out as I felt then, I never tried to make a "me vs. her" situation.

I know a lot of dads get into uncomfortable situations with their kids when they start dating women who aren't Mom. Everything is new and unusual to the kids; they just got here. Anelise's head is always on a swivel, taking in everything she sees, assessing. What is the meaning of life? How do magnets work? Where does the mail come from? This is how kids are, they are sponges, taking it all in. Even at a young age she could see how unique our family situation was.

Family drama goes into overdrive around the holidays. Sometimes it's simple to keep things separate. "Hey, you get this weekend, I'll take next weekend." Easy. But with holidays, there's only one day. (With some exceptions of course—"Hey, you take the first four nights of Hanukkah, I'll take the last four. Mazel tov!") So on New Year's Eve, you might have to bring everyone together, which is exactly what we did a few years ago. I know that kind of mixed celebration doesn't work for everyone, so I consider myself blessed that my family has figured out a way to not only get together without any drama, but to have a great time making new memories with each other. I always wanted my daughters to see that all the different families could be together. I can remember little Eric Bishop sitting around, praying and hoping that his mom and his family would come around, and here were all of us, with our own definitions of what family meant and, most important, together.

NOW I'M RAISING MY . . .
PARENTS?!

When it comes to things like divorce, breakups and new partners, there's definitely a difference in the way it gets handled on the white side of town and the hood side of town. I call it the cul-de-sac life versus the hood life. On the white side of town, with my white friends and other buddies that were well-to-do, when their parents got divorced, they sat them down and had a conversation that went something like this:

"Billy . . . Donovan . . . Ian . . . Tiffany . . . Listen, Mommy and Daddy are no longer going to be with each other. We still love you. We're getting a divorce and are going to venture into other relationships. But we wanted to check with you first to make sure you are centered and you're okay with it. If you want to voice any opinions about our relationship, we are open to that. You can go to Dad's therapist or Mom's therapist or the family therapist. Anyway, we just wanted to let you know that. Kisses!"

In the hood, shit is all different. You don't get the nice sit-down cul-de-sac talk. This is how you find out your mom is seeing another person or has married somebody you haven't even met:

You walk into the kitchen and you see a dude standing there, all hairy, with a medium-size Afro—Note to self: Never trust a person with a medium-size Afro—wearing your mom's robe, which is barely covering his ass, with his balls maybe glimmering just a little bit in the refrigerator light. But you can't be too sure about the balls 'cause you're afraid to look down—hey, you're just getting used to your own genitalia.

He turns around and says, "Wassup, little nigga? I'm your new daddy."

#WhatInTheAbsoluteFuckJustHappened.   That's how I met my mom's second husband. That's all I'm going to say about him.

My mother's third husband, George Dixon, is the man I call my stepfather. I also call him "Pops." I ended up spending more time with my mom once Pops came into the picture, and he turned out to be one of the biggest male influences in my life. He is a throwback, an old-school grown man who taught me much about how men should conduct themselves out in the world and in the home. He and my mother had two daughters, Deidra and DeOndra.

Pops treated me like I was his own son. He spent many hours with me on the tennis court, teaching me the fundamentals of the game. I got fairly good at tennis but I never understood the scoring method. In case you aren't familiar with it, the first time you score, you get 15, then you go up to 30, and then you go up to 40. Why not just count 1, 2, 3? And if you're already counting by fifteen, why then switch to adding ten? I don't fucking know! But I do know Pops got sick of me asking. Also, when you don't have any points in tennis, you aren't at zero . . . you're at "love." "What's up with that?" I'd often ask Pops. His answer? "It means, even when you think you ain't got nothing in this world, you still got love." Damn. Tennis was deeper than I thought.

Pops believed if I could play tennis I would be more comfortable in the elite circles where I one day hoped to socialize—it was his version of the piano my grandmother insisted I learn to play. The time and energy he invested in molding me felt so dramatically different than the brief encounters I had with my biological father over the years.

But he wasn't just a great influence on me.

Pops was a natural leader who tried to help everybody who needed it. He worked at a school, where he was a beloved and influential figure who impacted many kids' lives. You remember Edward James Olmos in *Stand and Deliver*? That was basically him, taking badass little gangbangers and making them learn algebra. He brought in people from the community to talk to the kids, to help them make connections to the outside world. They ranged from ballplayers to accountants—just people to show the kids as many options as he could. One of his regular speakers was a white judge who would warn the kids that they didn't ever want to be standing in his courtroom because that would mean they were heading in the wrong direction.

And very sadly, in the '80s, Pops himself got derailed as the wheels of the crack epidemic were rolling through every hood. Both my stepfather and my mother got caught up in the spokes of that and became addicts.

Like the men in her life, my mother had her own challenges over the years, many of which I was shielded from. I didn't know my mother had a drug problem until my late teens. We once had a nasty argument when I returned to Terrell to visit my grandmother not long after I moved to California. I saw she was living in my grandmother's house after she swore she would never move back. I accused her of taking advantage of my grandmother. Tempers flared up, emotions spilled over. It ended with her saying, "Why don't you just get the hell out of here?"

This was the first time I allowed myself to lash out. I wanted to make her feel some of the pain I had been feeling for years. I responded, "Why don't you just go to hell?"

My heart sank and tears flooded my eyes when she yelled back, "I'm already in it!" I was forced to think about my mother's perspective instead of my own. In that moment I said to myself, *When I get on, I'm going to fix this.*

A few years later, I started getting on with *In Living Color* and was making a name for myself. I felt like I was on the precipice of fame. But when things are going well in life, always watch your blindside. One day, I got a call from my sister Deidra, who was only about twelve at the time.

"Mommy and Daddy are not doing well," she said. She held back her tears, describing to me how they were not tending to the basic responsibilities of parenting her and DeOndra.

"You don't know what you're talking about, Deidra," I said, in denial. I didn't want to believe what my sister was telling me, but I quickly realized she wasn't lying.

When I went to try to find them in Dallas, the house they were supposed to be living in was occupied by someone else. What the hell? I called Deidra and apologized for not believing her, and I got the address of where they were at. I couldn't believe where they were living or, worse yet, *how* they were living. They were in a burned-out apartment—a place that looked like a scene from any '80s movie about the crack epidemic. There's "fucked up" and then there's "really fucked up!" They were taking refuge in the latter.

This wasn't the movies; it was live and I could see it right before me. These were my real parents. My mom, the lady who would wow the people in church, now looked painfully skinny and mute. She had such a wild and fun sense of humor that un-doubtedly rubbed off on me, but on this day she was a shell of the woman that I had known. My step-father, who had taught me how to play tennis and so many other things, sat there all discombobulated. It was like we were trapped in a Jordan Peele horror film and these two people were drugged-out clones of my mother and stepfather.

I spent days pleading with them and trying to convince them to go into treatment to beat the ad-diction, but they weren't ready yet. I couldn't force them. That's the thing with addicts: They need to get to a place where they want to help themselves.

I just hoped that when they finally were ready, it wouldn't be too late. Thank God, my grandparents stepped in yet again to help Deidra and DeOndra. I returned to LA, shaken by what I had seen.

Not long after, my stepfather, this man who had done so much for the community, landed in jail—for twenty-five dollars of illegal substance. I was completely devastated. I didn't think he needed jail time; he needed help. That very same judge who was a regular at his school was the judge who presided over his case and sent him to prison—which is pretty fucked up if you ask me.

At that time, I didn't want to go see him. I viewed him as a king; it would be too painful to see him behind bars. I wrote him a letter telling him I couldn't visit him in jail, but when he got out I would take care of him. It was such a devastating time for our whole family, and I thought about Pops and his story a lot when I was doing the film *Just Mercy*, which focuses on Bryan Stevenson's incredible work advocating on behalf of wrongly imprisoned inmates. I played one of his clients, Walter McMillian, whose freedom Bryan was able to secure. It was easy for me to sink into Walter's character because of what happened to Pops. I didn't come at the character from the perspective of an inmate. I would think about his family, about what he did for his community...and then I thought about the pain that went along with unjustly losing all that.

Unfortunately, one of the casualties of Pops's prison term was his relationship with my mother. It was just too much on her—visiting was tough. She was struggling to make ends meet, and now she also needed to put money on *his* books? Eventually the pressure and distance of prison proved too much and they divorced.

After a few years in prison, my stepfather got out shortly before 9/11. As I had promised him when he was in prison, I was ready to pull him in close. I told him, "Things are going good for me now. I worry about you when you're out of my sight. I want you to come live with me."

I could tell that his spirit had been broken, but he was looking for another chance and I was more than happy to provide him with that. I wanted to help him make up for those lost years. One of our special moments when he first got out was when I surprised him and took him to the US Open, a few days before 9/11. (This is not a story related to 9/11, but like most people I always seem to remember things as before and after that.) We sat there watching Venus and Serena play, with tears streaming down our faces, because tennis was always a special bond between us.

It was always a struggle over the years to connect

the emotional dots with my mother. Once I had a little Hollywood success and could afford it, I would send her plane tickets every year with the message: *If you would ever like to come out and hang with me, I would love to have you.* Occasionally she would take me up on it—but just like in church in Texas, she would blow in, make a quick connection and then abruptly be gone. I tried not to hold it against her, but being more mature now, I realized you do make the time for the people you truly love.

Then one day, about fourteen years ago, my mother accepted the plane ticket and flew out to hang with us for Christmas. My stepfather had already been living with me for about seven years and I was loving seeing them together, getting along. My mother's birthday was on December 31, so I knew she would stay until January 1, but...

January 2 came. She's still here.

January 14. Still here.

Valentine's Day—I got flowers for her—she was still around. *Hmmm.*

Saint Patrick's Day came and went but she hadn't. I had to pinch myself (not because I wasn't wearing green). I asked, "Mom, what you trying to say? You been here for a minute, and you ain't itching to get nowhere else?"

"Why? I can't hang out?" she said calmly. Being her Capricorn self—they can be stoic in the way they function when it comes to emotional things—this was the equivalent of her shouting from the mountaintops: "I want to show you how much I love you!"

When Mom agreed to stay, I was overjoyed. Growing up as an only child, I always wanted a big family. Anyone who knows me well will tell you that I love to always be surrounded by people. I used to watch *The Brady Bunch* and be like, *That shit looks hella fun with all those brothers and sisters running around.* Years later, I felt lucky to have my two daughters, but I didn't feel like I had the Brady Bunch–size family of my dreams. I wanted all the family members that were close to me under one roof.

That's not to say it can't get a little hairy at times. It's been a fascinating journey, having my mother and stepfather living in the house with me. Let me paint this picture for you. This is straight out of a sitcom (if my manager is reading this right now, remind me to pitch *this* show to Netflix). The word "complicated" doesn't even begin to describe the dynamic between Mom and Pops. These two have been married and then divorced and now are butting heads in the same house once again. The house is very big (thank you, *Collateral* and *Django* residuals), and my friends even refer to it as the Black Mansion. My parents even have separate wings, which you'd think would be enough to keep the peace, but they *still* manage to get in each other's way. So it maybe wasn't such a great idea to put them together under the same roof.

The worst of it revolves around Pops's dating life. My mom sometimes will sneak over to his side of the house when he has a date, to see what's going on and maybe kick up a little dust. He will inevitably come knocking on my door. "Hey, look here, you gotta tell her to stay off my side of the house." And I tell him, "You're both grown! You figure it out between the two of you!"

What is beautiful is that they still spend time together—they even go out sometimes. Like I said, "complicated." It's the most functional dysfunctional scenario and a crazy, improbable conclusion to their relationship.

"We old as a muthafucka now, we might as well just enjoy each other's company," Pops told me one day. "We ain't fin to be in bed with each other, we might as well have a good time."

It's good to see them this way after the hell they've been through. I vowed to get my mother out of her circumstances when I got on, and I'm glad I didn't have to break that promise.

It's like I'm raising my parents now. I'm so grateful both of my daughters are getting to spend such incredible quality years with their grandparents. The interactions between them really span the spectrum.

Sometimes it's serious, like recently on a boat trip, when Corinne's grandfather told her about his experiences as a Black man living in the South, dealing with police. She was already involved with Black Lives Matter, but she got to learn a lot from his perspective. And sometimes these interactions are funny as all hell, like when Corinne's grandmother got her a Subway gift card for Christmas (with a note that said HAPPY BIRTHDAY). I believe she got a turkey sub on the parmesan cheese bread. I already told you she isn't a Mr. Chow's girl.

BILLIE EILISH ALSO RAISES MY DAUGHTER

People say that you should bring your children to work with you to give them a window into what it is that you do. And yeah, I bring my kids around set where they can see a movie being made (and how slow and boring it can get). But that's just one facet of my job and life. The real window into what I do is right at home where I cultivate a creative space and people with brilliant minds roll through and share their gifts. Warning though: I'm gonna drop some big names in this chapter. I'm not trying to flex about who I know, but I just happen to be friends with a lot of famous people.

When friends and celebrities are going through something, they often come straight to my house.

I've tried to create a space where people feel like they can let down their guards. I'm like the comedic, Black version of Dr. Phil. Chadwick Boseman sat on the steps of my crib with his head in his hands right before the release of *Black Panther*, overwhelmed by the immensity of the moment. The biggest movie in the world was about to come out, but he was trying to figure life out. Michael B. Jordan was here too, right in the middle of the craziness that began to swirl around him when he became a star.

I tell them, "Hey, in our business, the only thing that matters is two words: 'action' and 'cut.' All the things that happen outside of those two words are yours. Go on and live your life. All the other stuff that's going to happen, it's just going to happen."

What it all comes down to is cultivating creativity and art, building an environment where creative people feel comfortable enough to be free, to drop the walls they've constructed over the years to protect themselves.

Corinne saw Ed Sheeran sleeping on my couch as he was blowing up. She learned two things: (1) what helps creativity is a safe environment where that creativity is nurtured, and (2) beautiful music and art can come from totally normal people who, like Ed, also accidentally get mustard stains on their shirts.

I live relatively far from LA, but Quincy Jones still loves coming to my place to talk. I can hear him now: "Hey, Jamie, man, I love coming here man, shit." Denzel Washington. Rick Ross. 2 Chainz. The list goes on—celebrities that my daughters have seen hanging at my place, being themselves. They have seen how their brains work, how they talk out ideas. It's not just a muse that comes in and gives a song-writer a hit song. Creativity is work, work, work. The muse rewards you for putting in the work. (Remember that Jay-Z quote from earlier?)

It's important for my daughters to see that, to see the creative process as raw and real…not just the finalized version that's presented to the public. Anelise has been witness to so many conversations about art that it was easy to bond with her about it. I once was able to forge a deeper connection with Anelise analyzing Billie Eilish, the incredibly talented pop star who is her favorite singer—or at least was at the time of this writing. Hey, it's a little girl's prerogative to change her mind.

"Billie Eilish is raising you—and it's okay," I said to her one day. "It's okay that Billie Eilish is who you love, but you're still ten. So I got to let you know that I have to be careful what goes into you, because if Billie Eilish is singing about, you know, troubled things or depression and everything, I just have to make sure you understand what that is, because once stuff goes in you, it becomes part of you."

"What do you mean?"

"Prince was my Billie Eilish," I said. "Everybody liked Michael Jackson because it was clean, it was family. But Prince was talking about sex."

Her eyes widened. "Whaaat?"

"Yeah," I said, nodding my head. "And my grandmother was like, 'That nigga is the Devil.' I said, 'Granny, it's alright.' Unlike how I could take your phone away from you or disable your iTunes, we're talking about albums. The *1999* album that I owned had frequent flyer miles because my grandmother would constantly go in, take the album off the stereo and fling that motherfucker out in the front yard. So I'm constantly buying the album over and over with the little money that I did have."

Anelise was giggling, hanging on every word.

"My grandmother said, 'I tell you, he's the Devil.' I said, 'Granny, he ain't the Devil.' She said, 'I'm telling you, that little nigga got hooves. He's Satan.'"

Now Anelise was cracking up. I leaned in. I told her how I used to listen to the Prince album when nobody was home, lying on the floor in the living room while it played on my grandmother's big stereo console—the kind where you taped a nickel to the needle to keep the record from skipping. My main chore after I got home from school was to clean the house. When I was done, I would get into my music. One day I was playing Prince over and over again, sinking deep into his musical and lyrical genius. To a budding fifteen-year-old musician in Terrell, his *1999* album was a revelation. But when the song "1999" came on, I freaked out a little bit. For the first time, I listened closely to the weird, distorted, deep voice that speaks at the start of the song.

"Don't worry, I won't hurt you," the voice says, sounding quite demonic. "I only want you to have some fun."

What the fuck? Why hadn't I noticed how scary it sounded? I thought, What if my grandmother was right—maybe he *is* the Devil. I started getting paranoid. Just then, my grandmother walked into the living room.

"What is this nigga doin'?!" she said, listening. Then she reached into the stereo and yanked out the album.

"Granny!" I said, trying to protest.

But she could not be stopped. In an instant, it was flying across the room like a black vinyl Frisbee. She sat down and started talking, giving me an insight into her thinking.

"Listen. Every generation has some music or something that they're doing that the parents don't like. I just got to make sure you understand what this guy's saying. I want you to understand what you're getting from him. If he's talking about sex, do you know about that? Because I don't want you following something that you hear on the record and maybe you gettin' a girl pregnant or maybe you gettin' something from a girl or you're doing some shit that this person is telling you to do." I couldn't tell Anelise what my grandmother went on to say—"So when he talkin' about threesomes, you try to have a threesome, you gonna be in jail for attempted rape." I knew the conversation had suddenly gotten real when Granny started talking to me about threesomes.

I had decided early on that it would be hypocritical or disingenuous if I tried to shield my daughters from my somewhat colorful language. I've always wanted them to know exactly who their father is. I'm a comedian; I'm a Black man; I talk a gang of shit. And I know they hear much worse from their friends anyway.

I realized maybe I was worrying too much about this pop singer. But isn't it my job as a parent to worry? A mother and father shape their kids, but their environment raises them. I can do my best to steer Anelise, but someone like Billie Eilish could tell her what to feel about depression or being gay or suicide. So I wanna do my best to frame those thoughts. But Anelise calmed my concerns.

Anelise nodded. "Dad, I get it. I know it's metaphorical."

I looked at her closely. Damn, did my eleven-year-old just say "metaphorical"? Damn, I guess having her be surrounded by artists made her appreciate art in a deeper, nonliteral way.

"Why do you like her?" I asked.

"Because it just seems like she's herself."

"Well, can I tell you something too?" I said. "Billie Eilish is not necessarily what you see. You always have to understand that there is a Wizard of Oz to everything in life. There's somebody behind the curtain who's orchestrating what they want you to see—whether it be on social media or in music."

Anelise came up to me later and said, "Wow."

"What's up?"

"I really dug that conversation," she said. "I don't like having those kinds of conversations that much, but I really understood it."

And our relationship over art only deepened. A little while later we discovered we both were sick with colds, and even though she didn't feel well, Anelise wanted to take care of me. She changed the humidifier and kept checking on me. We decided to sit down and write songs together.

"Dad, you don't mind if my song is dark, right?" she said, obviously thinking about our Billie Eilish conversation. Have I mentioned that my daughter *loves* Billie Eilish?

"Listen, this is what I want you to understand," I said. "You're still an artist, whether you're eleven or twenty-one or thirty-four. So I'm not telling you to not listen to Billie Eilish and cut your art off. I want you to listen and take in everything Billie Eilish has, but I just want to be able to hold you by your legs as you dip into whatever this is. And if it inspires you, I will be right there with you."

"Okay. Yeah, because my stuff is kind of dark."

"Well, let me hear it."

She started reading it to me. With each line, my heart swelled bigger and bigger, the pride overtaking me. That's my girl.

My shadow follows my every move
If I get a bruise she gets a bruise
Not all the things I do you can see
And yet she's still a part of me
I don't pay attention sometimes I lose track
My shadow does wicked things behind my back
When I smile at her, she doesn't smile at me
When I frown at her, she smiles with glee

My shadow wreaks havoc some say she's odd
My shadow is sinful it wouldn't please God
My shadow is sneaky she's also mean
I say she's guilty but maybe it's me

The dopeness overwhelmed your boy. But she wasn't done yet. The next one she wrote was even darker, scarier.

I woke up saw him staring right at me
he was so tall I tried hard not to scream
had no shoulders
as I walked over it got colder
Didn't have a lot of hair
tried to see what he might wear

closed six doors cause I was afraid
that those six doors might lead to my grave
Was tall and thin as a needle
dead man standing guarding the door to evil

Head floats with a creepy smile
Something about him seems really vile
Smile of a demon face of a troll
Pitch black darkness for the eyes of his soul
He attacks you mentally that's just the start
Rips your chest open there goes your heart

Closed six doors cause I was afraid
that those six doors might lead to my grave
was tall and thin as a needle
dead man standing guarding the door of evil

Who's that standing over me thought my door
    was locked
Holding my breath clutching my chest now I'm
    frozen in shock

As he gets closer I can smell his rotten stench
Yet I didn't blink I didn't move and I didn't flinch
He starting to get scared he's falling apart
Because he knows he can't scare me I'm already dark

She said the description of the man in the poem was a vision she saw in her room at night.

"You were dreaming?"

"No, Dad, I was awake," she said.

My eyes widened. "You sure?" Maybe my ears widened too. *Did I hear this girl right?*

She nodded. "I was awake, Dad. He was right there in the room. I wasn't scared. I love horror films."

I said, "Wow, okay." Maybe she wasn't scared but I sure as hell was.

She grinned at me. "Can we re-create it?"

"Huh?"

Anelise knows I hate everything about horror films; they just cause me crazy anxiety, like I need to mainline Xanax to get through them. Anelise forces me to watch them with her. She's always checking on me, asking if I'm okay. I'll answer, "No, no, no, no, I'm good. I'm a man!" But inside I'll be wailing like a big brown baby. I did love *A Quiet Place* though. But only the quiet parts, of course. Did not like it when it got loud.

With extreme, serious, overwhelming reluctance, I followed her direction and climbed up on a chair in her room. She drew me a picture of what the monster looked like. I summoned all my ability to impersonate the giant man in Anelise's dream-not-dream—all the while trying not to frighten my damn self.

The way my grandma pushed me to learn piano, I pushed Anelise. Except I could actually play, so I would teach her myself. When a dad teaches his kid how to do something, it creates a deep bond. And, if I'm being honest, I also was looking for those bragging rights. I would be able to score points forever if for the rest of her life she told people her father taught her how to play. I felt the same way about teaching her how to swim. For the rest of Anelise's life she will tell people her father taught her how to swim. That makes my chest stick out a little bit farther. Same goes for brushing her teeth, but usually people aren't impressed if you know how to do that. Unlike playing the piano.

Teaching piano was a delicate operation from day one. I didn't want to push too hard, particularly knowing how sensitive Anelise is about this stuff. It was a long-standing struggle between us. I tried to combine the two approaches—show her the notes but also show her how to play the songs she likes, by some of her favorite artists (back to that Billie Eilish). At one point I noticed that she seemed somewhat subdued whenever she was around the piano.

"What's wrong?" I asked. "Why you seem so... down?"

She shrugged. "Why is it that when you play the piano everybody sits around and listens? Then when I play piano no one comes around. I feel like I'm not being seen."

Damn. That was a tough one. I took a deep breath.

"Well, you know, Anelise, if you want people to crowd around, you have to really play well." I watched her face to make sure I wasn't crushing dreams or anything.

"When I hear you playing, I'm not sure if you want to be bothered. I tell myself, 'Let Anelise do her thing.'" I looked at her and smiled. "I will make sure I come in and listen to you next time."

And to encourage her, I told her, "If you play well enough, maybe we'll send it to Billie Eilish."

I had a big party at my crib for my birthday in December 2019. As I'm sure I've made clear by now, I don't cheat myself when it comes time to party. Never have. I throw myself in, dive into the deep end of that motherfucker. I take up a whole lot of space. And this party had a whole lot of people take up a whole lot of space. Even Drake was there. Who Anelise loved almost as much as Billie Eilish. She once even told me, "Drake is my boyfriend."

I saw Drake on the balcony and I went over

to him. "Every time you come here, you got to perform," I said.

"Well, what should I do?" he asked.

"Sing something."

He leaned over the balcony and started singing the opening lines from "Find Your Love," the Kanye West–written and –produced hit from Drake's debut album.

I'm more than just an option
Refuse to be forgotten

The crowd went crazy. But that still wasn't the biggest hit of the night. The party was raging hard and heavy, the *boom boom* of the latest hit record rattling the walls. I heard something else playing in the background, the light tinkling of notes that sounded a lot like "The First Noel."

What is that?

I looked over in the corner and saw that it was Anelise. She was playing the piano as loud as she could, trying to attract a crowd. It was working— the party started to gather around her. I heard people complimenting her on her playing.

It was delicious vindication for Anelise—and for me. She might as well have been center stage at Carnegie Hall, as enormous as that scene was for the Foxx household. I let her soak up the attention for a while, giddy as hell. Then I sat down with her and we played together for more than an hour. It was glorious.

"How did you learn that?" somebody asked her.

"My dad taught me," she said.

My heart swelled so big, I almost spontaneously combusted right there on the piano bench.

She's becoming me, I thought later that night. Sports. Music. Writing. She doesn't even know it yet, but she's me. Also, for the record, Billie Eilish is amazing.

TRIPPIN' OUT

*D*rugs. That's the scary word. That's what you don't want your kids to get mixed up in. And hopefully they don't. And if they do, hopefully it's a little sip of wine with dinner. But it's a wild world and you gotta be ready for anything.

Corinne went through an episode when she was a teenager. Don't worry, she didn't have to go to rehab and we didn't have to drug test her every two weeks. But as a parent, it was still horrifying! She was at a party and somebody slipped her a cookie that had been infused with THC. Before you think that I'm overreacting, that it was just weed, I wanna take you back to my college years, where a drug episode fucked me up for a long time.

I didn't start smoking weed until the summer after I graduated from high school, right before I went to college. I was like, *Damn, this is what I've been missing?!* So I went in hard, making up for lost time, smoking practically every day that summer. When I got to California, I was around a new set of people. I didn't know many of them, but I certainly was open to new experiences. I was hanging with some friends and this dude gave us a little bag of stuff. I was all in. We smoked up the loose weed that was in the bag first, not messing with the rolled joint that was already in there. But after we were high, I pulled out the rolled joint. *Yo, let me try this shit.* I knew nothing about the dude who gave it to us besides his name. At the time, I felt indestructible.

Shortly after I smoked that joint, I noticed something was off. I was used to being high on weed, but this was different. I would look at a painting and it would start moving. I'd look down at my hands and the lines would start moving. I told my friend something was wrong, and he said, "Oh, you didn't know that was laced with LSD?" No, motherfucker, I did *not* know I was taking acid! Now I was stuck on *The Love Boat*, headed for Looney Land and unable to get off the boat.

"I feel like I'm drowning!" I told my friends. When I looked like I couldn't even talk anymore, they ran and got more of my homies. They rushed me to the hospital. I eventually came down off the high, but my head was still fucked up. I started praying, "God, if you let me get through this...Please, Lord."

When I made it back to my room, I slept all day. I got up to go to dinner, feeling okay. I thought it was over. But at the table I leaned back in my chair and suddenly hit the floor. I started having flashbacks, my mind tripping again like it was the previous night. My roommate, a white guy from Nebraska, was an immense help to me. He would talk to me as I was struggling, like a lifeline back to sanity. Looking back, I realize his advice was just good common sense, but at the time, things like "Hey man, you need to drink some water" and "Change your posture, sit upright" seemed brilliant. That was especially helpful because the homies I talked to were telling me all the wrong shit.

"You need to get back on your shit and smoke some more to bring you back down, nigga. That's what you need to do. You need to bite the hair of the dog, fool." Yeah, that's it. To get out of a drug hole, what you need is more drugs. That's like treating a hangover by getting drunk again. Which people do...a little hair of the dog.

So I tried it—I smoked more weed. And it felt like my head was about to pop off my body like a Pez dispenser. What the fuck! I was back to where I started, having all kinds of wild hallucinations. I started convincing myself that maybe it wasn't even the drugs, maybe I was actually going crazy! In my high state, I would try to logic myself into figuring it out. I would say to myself, *If I get up and go in the closet, then I'll know I'm crazy.* The next thing you know, I'd be standing in the closet, wondering how I got there. But then I would think, *Well, if I knew I was getting in the closet, then I can't be crazy.*

I don't want this book to turn into a D.A.R.E. pamphlet, but if you're ever thinking about dropping acid, you should know it might not just be a one-day experience. My flashbacks were lasting days. I stopped going to class, I stopped eating. I looked like I was wasting away. I got the idea in my head that there was only one place where I could get back to normal— Terrell, Texas, in the household of Estelle Talley.

The twenty-six-hour drive from San Diego to Texas was tough. At times I would think there were dudes sitting in the car next to me and I'd get all paranoid. I couldn't see them but I could sense them. I drove straight through. I would have moments when I was panicked and freaked out, but then I'd have periods when I was in a zone for hours, just zooming along without any worries.

When I walked into my grandmother's house, I was overcome with emotion. There's something about seeing a familiar face in times of distress that can overwhelm you.

"Boy, what's wrong with you?" my grandmother said when I started sobbing.

"Granny, I'm just so happy to see you!" I said.

"You ain't happy to see me. What's wrong with you?"

"What you mean?" I asked her.

"Let me look in your eyes. I know you ain't on them drugs!"

When she said the word "drugs," it was like a trigger was squeezed. The word echoed in my head, bouncing around like a pinball. *Drugs. Drugs. Drugs.* I started thinking, *Oh shit, she can see it!*

"Well, are you on drugs, nigga?" she asked. Just picture Madea interrogating me and you have a precise image of what it looked like.

"No, Granny. No, I'm not." Not anymore, Granny. I'm just having flashbacks of when I *was* on drugs.

She sat me down and she cooked me a big breakfast. But I still had no appetite. I forced down a few bites when she was watching me, but when she turned her back I dumped it in the trash. She told me she needed some stuff from the grocery store and asked if I could go for her. Even the trip to the store, one I had taken many times, felt like a crazy journey. It was a weekday in the middle of the afternoon, so there was nobody in the store. I went down the aisles looking for the few items she needed, like chicken broth. Christmas was approaching, so Granny was gearing up, getting ready to go in. I turned a corner on one of the aisles and saw a familiar face. It was Miss Williams, who had been one of my piano teachers when I was younger. Miss Williams wore enormous bifocals that had a bit of a tint. When I gazed at her, I swore that she looked like the Fly, the character from that old horror movie. I stared at her and could swear I heard the sound of a giant fly buzzing in my head. *Bzzzzz!!* I tried to get past her, but she spotted me right away.

"Hey son, how are you?" she asked with a warm smile.

"Umm, I'm good, Miss Williams."

"Well, it's good to see you." She looked me up and down. "You in college now. Boy, you need to eat. You need some food in you."

I nodded. It was all I could do to stop myself from running. "Yes, ma'am. I'm just eating healthy and everything now. You know how California is."

She nodded and looked at me more closely.

"Well, I'm glad you doin' good in that college. And you know what? I really appreciate that you ain't messin' with no drugs!"

Noooo! Again the word bounced around in my head. *Drugs. Drugs. Druuuuugggss.*

"Alright, Miss Williams. Good to see you."

I got out of there as fast as I could. Soon after I got home, I decided to say my goodbyes and drive all the way back to San Diego. When I got to school, my roommate was a lifesaver once again. He would talk me to sleep from the bottom bunk. "Everything is cool," he'd say. "You're on the top bunk. We're here at college. Everything is great." He would keep saying simple declarative sentences like that to keep me calm until I went to sleep. I give him a great deal of credit for being a mental breadcrumb of sorts, helping to lead me back to normalcy. What I mostly needed was for time to pass. But goddamn was it scary before it passed!

So when I got the call about Corinne, I was expecting the worst. When her mother called me, frantically explaining that Corinne had gone on some kind of drug trip and was in the hospital, I tried not to panic. I told her I would handle it.

"Hey kiddo, how you doin'?" I said when I arrived in her room.

"Dad, I was in a bad place," she said.

"I know," I said. "They checked your system. It was just weed."

I told her I reacted differently than most people to weed and other drugs. Perhaps she was the same way.

"Well, at one point I felt like I wanted to jump off the balcony," she said, her eyes widened.

When I heard that, it confirmed for me that she had gone through the same type of experience I did in college. And I remembered how scary it felt back then, thinking I was alone or something was wrong with me. So I told her, "Aww, come on. It's just a drug. That's what drugs do." Nothing wrong with you. If you take NyQuil, you'll get sleepy. You take some crazy shit, you'll think some crazy shit.

I told her that our minds have something that operates like a trapdoor to keep all those scary thoughts at bay. "When you do drugs, it pushes the door ajar and some of those little creepy things jump out," I said. "It was a little weed; you're going to be fine. But I am going to stay with you tonight."

"Why?" she asked.

"Because the boogeyman is coming," I said.

I didn't wanna scare her. I just wanted to lighten the mood a bit. She did eat the brownie by accident after all. "You just have to hang in there," I said. And I stayed with her, like my old roommate did with me.

This was the first time I was actually glad I had that bad acid trip. They say what doesn't kill you makes you stronger, but what doesn't kill you also gives you insight into helping your kids when they make mistakes. And if you happen to be reading this book in the middle of a bad acid trip, remember to change your posture to be upright, drink lots of water and put on some nice music. Acid can really make your brain snowball, so if you keep pushing happy thoughts, eventually you will become happy thoughts. And if you're telling yourself to get into the closet to prove you are or aren't crazy, don't get into the closet.

FEMINISM, REALISM, AND A LITTLE POLE DANCING

The other day I was talking about hip-hop with Anelise and we got to the message in the lyrics. I was proud when she looked at me and asked, "They're calling women bitches—am I a bitch?" She was telling me that she rejected the notion that was being peddled in the music. The words, the message, the intent, were not okay. Sometimes we get too used to these things because they're all around us and we become desensitized.

Now, I'm a feminist, in the sense that I believe women are equal to men, should be paid the same as men, should be president, etc. I'm also a realist, so I can't turn a blind eye to the struggles women face in our society. A big part of raising girls is making sure you're empowering them, which means being honest with them about the challenges they will face and showing them that they have the ability to overcome them.

With Corinne and with Anelise, it's been so gratifying to me that all the lessons I've tried to impart about hard work and about how special they are have started to come to fruition. That's the job of dads, to fill them up with notions of nothing being too hard or impossible for them, no matter the circumstances, no matter what their thing is— acting, writing, basketball, track, singing, dancing, science. Corinne will say that I used to empower her so much that it felt weird—until she was on a set with Viola Davis and Tiffany Haddish, holding her own. Then she understood why I did it.

A quick little sidebar while on the topic of Tiffany Haddish. I think that she, along with many other female comedians, has proven beyond a shadow of a doubt that women are as funny as men. Oftentimes, funnier! However, the ugly lie that "women aren't as funny as men" has been a prevalent negative force in society, often preventing young women from pursuing comedy. Which indirectly resulted in my changing my name to Jamie Foxx. You see, back when I was just starting out as a comedian, I would regularly attend open mics. The thing about open mics is...they're open to all! So every time I'd sign up, I'd be signing up at the end of a list of a hundred people. And I started to notice that almost all of the names were male. More importantly, I noticed that the hosts made an effort to prioritize calling up the few women that did sign up that night. I started to feel like an Eric wasn't likely to get called—and I needed to get called if I was ever going to become famous! But hey, if I signed in with an androgynous name like a Stacy or a Traci or a...Jamie, suddenly I got called up to perform more regularly. Jamie Foxx was just a quick stage name I threw together, got called up, killed extra hard that night...and I guess it stuck.

Back to my girls. I think I have to be dogmatic with them, unrelenting. Even to the point where they might get sick of me. My grandma used to tell me, "Your kids ain't supposed to like you all the time. But they need to respect you." There are going to be days when the things we say to them aren't going to go down so easy. But we can't let up or back off. If they can't take it when I challenge them, how are they going to take it when it's a boss or some-body out in the world telling them some negative bullshit? Thank God things have recently started to evolve, but there's still a long way to go. Women deal with a lot more shit than men and they need to have a good sense of who they are so it doesn't stand in the way of their success.

I feel a constant pressure to pass on to my daughters everything that Estelle Talley passed on to me and more. I want them to be armed to the gills when they step out of my house. They're going to need every iota of self-esteem, every morsel of confidence, every bit of toughness. Because the minute they pass through the threshold and walk out the door, someone is going to try to tear it all down.

When Corinne was a teenager, she was invited to a sixteenth birthday party where they were planning to bring the girls to a place where they could learn to dance on a stripper pole. When I found out, I couldn't believe it. What the fuck is that? I called the parents and told them, "If you ever do that, I'll be on your doorstep. We're not stripping. We're not taking our clothes off. That shit ain't happening."

Yes, I know stripping has become mainstream, but for a sixteen-year-old's birthday?! As their dad, I need to be old-school, to stand up and say, "Hey! That ain't how it should go!" They don't need to get used to anybody calling them bitches, even if it is in a song.

No, in my household, my job is to let my daughters know, every moment of every day, that they can have everything in the world. Not just things connected to their physical appearance. There are already far too many pressures on them as it is to be beautiful. That's the world they will be living in.

So I need to find ways to empower my daughters that aren't just about looking good. They can be empowered by being tough and having the strength to stick with things until they develop mastery. And obviously sports has been a great venue to teach them this.

I felt I had made some progress with Anelise when I saw how she responded after a tough loss in basketball. Her elementary school cheering section wasn't there for this game—but my sister Deidra was. This was potentially even more nerve-racking for Anelise because she really wanted to show out for her aunt. In Anelise's mind, Deidra represents the hood of South Dallas, the swag and the glory of premium Blackness. She sees her aunt as tough, mean, even a bit scary. There's probably nobody on the planet she'd want to impress more than Deidra (other than me, I hope). But this was one of those games where it wasn't working out. She was getting increasingly frustrated on the court. I've seen her angry before, but this was on another level. She got really pissed that somebody had hit her in the stomach.

During a time-out, she announced angrily, "One thing I ain't gonna do is let nobody hit me in the stomach!" She had all kinds of extra sauce on the vowels and consonants, like she had sprinkled them with Lawry's.

She leaned in and told her teammates, "When

we go back out there, somebody do something to make a distraction and I'm gonna hit him back in the stomach." She said it quietly, conspiratorially, like she was the don working out a hit with her enforcer.

My eyes widened, but I didn't say anything—none of that parental "Oh, you should play nice" bullshit. Because I know what it feels like to be battling, to get frustrated and want a little bit of revenge. That's part of sport.

After the game, Anelise was distraught by how it turned out; they had lost and she hadn't performed well. And I don't think she got her revenge either. Just a sorry-ass day. Deidra went and wrapped her arms around Anelise—she had to reach up to do that, since Deidra is a hair under five feet and Anelise is taller than even me now. I saw the tears well up.

"You played a great game," Deidra said.

"I'm so mad!" Anelise said. "I'm so mad we lost."

I stepped away from the scene to let them have their moment. Deidra came to find me a bit later. "This is what I'm going to tell you about your daughter," she said. "She's tough. And she's angry."

"What did she say?"

"She said she's so mad, she doesn't know whether to kill her team or kill the other team. But either way, somebody gotta die today."

"Whaaaat?!" I said. "I'm feeling a lot of love for my daughter right now!" Unfortunately, in our society there is a stereotype about angry women—especially angry Black women. So I'm proud that I raised her not to be scared. To show who she is. I love her competitive spirit. Her response on that day let me know that she doesn't like to lose. We need to cultivate that. It's not something to take for granted—not every eleven-year-old girl is going to respond to losing by insisting that somebody's gotta die. Maybe a bit of a red flag, but I can be as passionate, so she gets it from me.

I had a special moment with Anelise a few days later that was like an exclamation point at the end of a profound sentence. We were watching ESPN in the morning and Stephen A. Smith was doing a tribute on his show to Stuart Scott, the late great ESPN anchorman who died of cancer in 2015. They played the video of Stuart onstage giving what turned out to be his final speech before he passed. It was an incredibly heartfelt, moving moment. In the speech, he said that to his daughters he isn't the great Stuart Scott, he's just Dad—sometimes a good guy, sometimes a tyrant. I looked at Anelise because it felt so relevant, and she burst out laughing.

"You see how a dad, even in his last moments, just wants to connect with his daughter?"

"Yeah," she said.

"Yeah, that's all it is. But remember that this dude is onstage, saying goodbye to the world, but he wanted to make sure that when he left, his daughters understood that everything he did was for them. That's why it caves me in when during the moments we do have together, we lose time," I said. "Like if we're at the gym or we're at the piano, and things don't go well, we lose those moments. That troubles me. I want to get that right."

She gave me a nod, like she totally got it. When we got in the car to go to school, it occurred to me that I had a way of even further solidifying the point. I could do it with music, since I knew music was an artistic pacifier for her, just like it was for me. I picked up my phone and I pulled up a Billie Eilish song on the Bluetooth. As we pulled out on the commute to school, Billie's voice filled every space in the car. I glanced at Anelise in the rearview mirror. She didn't see me, but she had a huge grin on her face. Billie was our soundtrack that morning, the glue connecting this father and his beloved daughter, putting words to an understanding between us, a deep and abiding love that didn't need to be voiced. It floated in the air between us, just like the music. Sweet and soulful and unforgettable.

Part of being a dad to daughters is knowing I won't always know all the struggles and frustrations that they'll face. I just gotta do my best to be aware and help where I can. And if asking for the biggest favor in the world from the biggest star in the world can make me a better father, so be it. (Thank you for the video, Billie. I still owe you!)

DAD STOP EMBARRASSING ME!

Needless to say, especially by this point in the book, my daughters and I have been through some shit. It was ironic how badly I wanted to go to Six Flags as a kid, because now I'm on a nonstop emotional roller coaster. And this roller coaster just recently went through a loop-de-loop known as *Dad Stop Embarrassing Me!*

The idea came about on one of those days where Corinne and I were just arguing about something stupid—I was trying to pull off skinny jeans and she wasn't having it. But then, while she was demanding I go change before being seen in public like that, she stopped. Like a switch flipped in her brain. "Dad," she said, "this...is a show."

"Yeah, yeah, I know, the Jamie and Corinne show."

But no. She meant a literal show. It took me a second longer but the same lightning bolt hit me too. *Goddamn, she's right!* All of our craziness and love and comedy could be a sitcom. And that's what it eventually became, currently streaming on Netflix (No. 1 show in the world, by the way!). Pop it on if you haven't. And don't use your co-worker's cousin's next-door neighbor's log-in. Support a brother and pay for your own damn Netflix.

I've been to therapy with Corinne, but damn did I learn a lot more making this show with her. She would go off—"My dad this, my dad that"— and I'd have to stop her and say, "You mean the *character* Brian this, Brian that." And then she'd tell a story about her fake ID and I'd stop the pitch again. "Hold up. *Your* fake ID?" And she'd hit me back with "Excuse me, the *character* Sasha's fake ID." I think our organic banter is what Netflix most responded to.

And this show felt like so many parts of my life were coming full circle (or semicircle, I ain't dead yet!). Thanks to my grandmother nurturing my creativity, I was able to have the tools to nurture Corinne's creativity, and now here we were, executive producers of a show together about our own life. And the show began to feel even more like family when I called up my man Bentley Kyle Evans, who co-created *The Jamie Foxx Show*, to showrun (which is Hollywood talk for being the head writer and overseeing everything else). And, if that wasn't enough, I went back to my *In Living Color* days and brought on David Alan Grier to play my Pops. He's only ten years older than me so I FaceTimed him and asked if he was insulted to be offered this role, but once I saw his gray beard, I told him, "Well, you're already on your way."

And I can't believe that after all that work raising Corinne, she's now my boss! And she runs a tight ship on the show. I can't be late, I gotta be on my best behavior, and she's the first one to tell me if a scene isn't funny or authentic. Because the core of the show has always been our relationship. Both good and bad. When people ask how much of the show is based on us, I tell them: She literally took her diaries and shared them with the writers' room. By the way, these are diaries I still have never seen! And never will, according to her. I once cornered this writer Wayne Stamps and was like "Tell me what's in those goddamn diaries." But before I could get it out of him, he suddenly needed to go to craft services and Corinne needed me in "hair and makeup" to get ready to "shoot a scene." Like I said, tight ship.

When you have people you trust and love working together in harmony, amazing things can happen.

Corinne revealed getting a fake ID to the writers' room, which clever writer Molly Kiernan combined with Corinne's social justice passion and turned it into a misunderstanding where the fake ID was actually for the character Sasha to try to vote (just some light voter fraud). Hotshot writer Alex Kavutskiy took my and Corinne's drug stories and added that, after finding the fake ID, my character was so panicked that his daughter was on drugs that he broke into her bedroom while she was sleeping to steal a hair sample and take it to the police for a drug test! And then Bentley Kyle Evans, the sitcom legend that he is, brought it all home with an epic intervention scene where me, David Alan Grier and the rest of the killer cast confront this poor girl and accuse her of being on every single drug known to man. Shooting this felt like I was back on *The Jamie Foxx Show*, and having Corinne there—and, more importantly, having Corinne laugh—meant everything to me.

I remember looking at Corinne behind the camera, smiling at me. I was so proud that I helped her to find her passion in acting and now I was helping her find her passion in producing.

And I looked over at Anelise, who was visiting set that day. She was cracking up every time David Alan Grier accused Sasha of being "on that blue magic!" I was watching her laugh and laugh, so proud that I was also helping her find her passion—and I can't wait to help her find a new one if she changes her mind. Right now she's into sports, into chess, but she's about to be a teenager and we know how that goes. One day she wants to be a doctor and the next she'll wanna be a NASCAR driver. And I'll be there to get her a stethoscope or be in her pit crew, changing her tires. All I can do is nurture and pass along any nuggets of wisdom I may have accidentally collected. Would I be thrilled if Anelise ended up being my boss on set someday? Absolutely. But what'll make me happier is being part of her journey to finding what makes her happiest. She still worships Billie, by the way.

As a dad, you're so often worried about everything. But every once in a while, you have a moment, like I did on set that day with my daughters, when you realize, "Damn, I did a few things right." When those moments come, give yourself permission to pat yourself on the back a little. Because the next crisis is probably coming around the corner. I always say, In the grocery store of life, whenever something good happens you will have to pay the price for it.

So this may be the last chapter in my book, but it sure as hell ain't the last chapter of my relationship with my daughters. I have plenty more parenting to do, I have plenty more fucking up to do, I have plenty more making up for the fucking up to do, etc.,

etc., etc. And hopefully one day (though maybe not that soon), I'll get to put my grandparenting skills to the test (that will probably be another book). For now, my girls and I will carry the baton of lessons and love my grandmother gave to me. From here to there, whatever it may be, Estelle Talley is with us. All of what you read, me here today writing this last chapter of this book, was sparked by the passion one lady had for me as a little, bigheaded baby. I'm so blessed to be where I am and with the people I am with. To my daughters, there are no guarantees in life but one thing I can definitely promise my daughters is... this dad will never stop embarrassing you.

ACKNOWLEDGMENTS

The author would like to acknowledge the following people in the making of this book.

First and foremost, Estelle and Mark Talley. My two beautiful daughters, Corinne and Anelise. My sister Deidra. The Dixon and Rosebud families. The city of Terrell, Texas. Everyone at Grand Central Publishing—Ben Sevier, Jimmy Franco, Amanda Pritzker and most important, my editor Suzanne O'Neill for her patience and belief. My cowriter, Nick Chiles, and the rest of the creative team: Alex Kavutskiy, Anthony Mattero and Dave Brown. Special shout-out to my friend of thirty years Bentley Evans. Thank you, Allison, Alan, Raquel and Eric. My guys Rick (Keyser), Ian, Chuck, Matt and James.

To my sister and angel DeOndra Dixon, thank you for holding your umbrella over me from up above.

—Jamie Foxx
June 2021

ABOUT THE AUTHOR

Jamie Foxx is an award-winning actor, singer and comedian. His accolades include an Academy Award for Best Actor, a BAFTA Award for Best Actor in a Leading Role, a Golden Globe Award for Best Actor in a Motion Picture—Musical or Comedy and a SAG Award for Outstanding Performance by a Male Actor in a Leading Role. He's also a Grammy Award–winning musician, having produced four albums that charted in the top ten in the United States. Most important, if you haven't read the book yet, he is the father to two daughters, Corinne and Anelise, that he loves very much.